Mark Graham Brown

► KEEPING
SCORE

Using the
Right Metrics
to Drive
World-Class
Performance

PRODUCTIVITY
productivity press

Productivity Press • New York

Productivity, Inc.
444 Park Avenue South, Suite 604
New York, NY 10016
United States of America
Telephone: 212-686-5900
Fax: 212-686-5411
E-mail: info@productivityinc.com

Library of Congress Cataloging-in-Publication Data

Brown, Mark Graham.
    Keeping score : using the right metrics to drive world-class performance /
  by Mark Graham Brown.
        p.   cm.
    Includes bibliographical references and index.
    ISBN 0-527-76312-8 (Quality Resources: alk. paper)
    ISBN 0-8144-0327-1 (AMACOM: alk. paper)
      1. Organizational effectiveness—Evaluation.   2. Industrial efficiency—Evaluation.
  3. Customer services—Evaluation.   4. Job
  satisfaction—Evaluation.   I. Title.
  HD58.9.B76   1996
  658.8'12—dc20   95-52139
                                                                      CIP

04 03 02   15 14 13 12

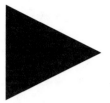

Contents

Acknowledgments   v

Introduction   vii

PART I: EVALUATING YOUR MEASUREMENT SYSTEM   1

1 Measurement: The Key to World-Class
   Performance   3

2 Problems with Most Measurement Systems   15

3 Evaluating Your Existing Measurement
   System   27

PART II: SELECTING THE RIGHT METRICS   39

4 Keeping Score in World-Class
   Organizations   41

5 Measuring Financial Performance   49

6 Measuring Customer Satisfaction
   and Value   59

7 Measuring Product/Service Quality   83

8   Measuring Processes and Operational
    Performance   95

9   Measuring Supplier Performance   111

10 Measuring Employee Satisfaction   123

PART III: REDESIGNING YOUR MEASUREMENT SYSTEM   139

11 How to Design Your Own Measurement System   141

12 Linking Measures to Strategy and Key
    Success Factors   159

13 Reporting and Analyzing Performance Data   171

14 Linking Measures, Goals, and Plans   179

Bibliography   193

Index   195

Acknowledgments

There are not many original ideas out there, and much of the conceptual material in this book is based on the ideas and writings of others. Robert Kaplan's and David Norton's "balanced scorecard" articles in the *Harvard Business Review* served as the foundation for many of the concepts in this book. In addition, I have drawn heavily on the work of Guy Hamel and C. K. Prahalad, whose books and articles on strategy are outstanding.

I am mostly indebted to my clients who have provided me with a wide variety of experience in actually designing and implementing measurement systems and developing plans. The individuals and companies to whom I wish to express my gratitude include the following:

— Marie Artale and Mark Carroll, IBM.

— Bijan Anvar and Dennis Pikop, Northrop Grumman.

— Mike Bennett and Craig Skrivseth, Appleton Papers.

— Jeff Heisler, Australia New Zealand Direct Lines.

— Roger Hessenius and Paul Aday, Ericsson.

— Larry Mercier, U.S. Coast Guard, Baltimore Yard.

— Vera Sadkovsky and Steve Welsh, Pacific Bell.

— Ray Serretti, Air Products and Chemicals.

Many individuals from Cargill gave me the opportunity to teach the concepts in this book to its senior managers all over the world. In working with this fine company over the past few years, I have learned that it is indeed possible to delight customers, make healthy profits, and be a company that employees are proud to work for. I have learned and developed a great deal of expertise by working with Dr. Carol Pletcher, Judy Aarness, Phil Forvé, Al Foster, Nat Jackson, Jodi Kohlenberger, Greg Meyer, Jerry Mogck, and Maureen Smith. I would also like to thank Charlene Reiss of the Forum Corporation for her suggestions on the manuscript.

This book is dedicated to my parents,
Donald and Joan Brown.

Introduction

Every day, thousands of managers and professionals in all types of organizations spend thousands of hours collecting, reading, and sitting in meetings listening to others review performance data. In fact, I would imagine that most managers and technical professionals spend at least 25 percent of their time reviewing data. This figure is probably even greater in large corporations. Is all of this time well spent? I doubt it. From my experience consulting with many major corporations and government organizations, I see a lot of time wasted looking at data that has questionable value to the running of the organization. Not only does this waste valuable management time, but looking at the wrong metrics can confuse decision making and lead to the wrong business decisions.

ALL ORGANIZATIONS COLLECT DATA

All organizations collect some type of data right now. This book is about how to make sure that you are measuring the right variables that will ensure your success both now and in the future. Spending some time thinking about what you currently measure and adding new measures to your database that help you track progress toward your future vision are what this book is all about. The basic premises of this book are that it is important to develop measures that focus on the past, present, and future; and that measures need to consider the needs of your customers, shareholders or owners, and your employees. The book is also based on the idea that it is worse to measure too many things than it is to not measure anything at all. Trying to track everything that may be of importance is a common problem in organizations. Convincing management to select the vital few key measures from the wide array of metrics that are currently tracked is a difficult task. Information is power, and many are reluctant to trust a few overall ratios or aggregate indices—they want the details.

HOW THE BOOK IS ORGANIZED

The book is divided into three parts. Each part focuses on a different aspect of measurement. Part I is about evaluating your current approach to measurement and the existing metrics on which you collect data. Chapter 1 provides an overview of the concepts on which this book is based. The measurement model presented herein is based largely on the work of Robert Kaplan and David Norton, and on the criteria of the Malcolm Baldrige National Quality Award. The Baldrige Award criteria have become a widely accepted set of standards for running an effective organization and they focus a great deal on selecting the right performance metrics. Companies that perform well with the Baldrige criteria as a group outperform their counterparts in the stock market by a wide margin. These organizations, like AT&T (a three-time Baldrige winner), have found that the emphasis on selecting a few key performance metrics linked to key success factors has allowed them to improve profits, achieve high levels of customer satisfaction, and become a better place to work for employees.

Chapter 2 presents a discussion of what organizations do wrong when measuring performance. It provides a variety of examples of metrics that drive the wrong performance and of measurement systems that do not focus on making an organization more successful. Chapter 3 is organized differently from any of the others. It is a self-assessment survey that allows you to evaluate how close your current measurement system is to the concepts presented herein. If you achieve a very high score on this survey, you may want to consider giving this book to a friend who works in an organization that isn't quite as enlightened as yours.

Part II contains chapters on selecting each of the major types of metrics on your organization's scorecard. Chapter 4 presents an overview of the different categories of data discussed in each of the remaining chapters. Chapter 5 is about how to select the right financial metrics. I discuss EVA, or economic value-added, as a new financial metric, but most of the chapter focuses on how to narrow your financial data to the vital few. Chapter 6 is the longest one in this part. It focuses on measurement of customer satisfaction and value. This is the area of most organizations' measurement systems that is the weakest. The emphasis in this chapter is on linking customer satisfaction and value measures with buying behavior. Chapter 7 is about how to measure the quality of your products and services before they reach your customers. Internal quality metrics are just as important as external customer satisfaction measures. Chapter 8 is about process measurement, along with other key operational measures like productivity, safety, and environmental performance. Many organizations spend more on buying goods and services from suppliers than they do on anything else. Tracking the performance of suppliers is of extreme importance in your overall scorecard; systems for doing this are described in Chapter 9. The final chapter in Part II addresses an area of measurement that is forgotten by many organizations—employee satisfaction. Information is presented on the right and wrong ways of measuring employee satisfaction and how to develop an overall employee satisfaction index that tells you about the overall well-being of your workforce.

The third part of the book is about how to actually redesign your metrics and the systems used to collect and report performance data in your organization. Chapter 11 presents a step-by-step model for designing a project to redesign your measurement system. This process can be applied to a single location or unit, or to the entire organization. Chapter 12 covers the most important concept in the book—linking your metrics to your key success factors. Key success factors are those variables that allow you to differentiate your organization from its major competitors. Select the wrong key success factors and you will develop the wrong metrics. Chapter 13 is a fairly straightforward discussion of how to report and make sense out of the performance data you decide to collect. The final chapter is about strategic planning. Measures without goals and strategies are not very useful; this final chapter presents an approach for developing annual and longer-term goals and plans to help you achieve your vision.

Part   I

Evaluating
Your
Measurement
System

Measurement: The Key to World-Class Performance

Great advances have been made in the medical field during the past 10 years with the discovery of better techniques for measuring certain chemicals that are found in the blood. Prostate-specific antigen, for example, is a very good predictor of future prostate problems and even cancer. The science of measuring and predicting organizational health seems to be sadly lagging behind the medical field, however. Many organizations today use the same bottom-line-oriented measures of performance that they did 30 or more years ago. Measuring the right variables has a lot to do with the likelihood of your future success. Just as better blood analyses have allowed doctors to predict and control health problems before they get out of hand, business executives need to use better data to lead their organizations on a successful path for the future.

This book is about how to rethink your approach to organizational measurement. Some characteristics of this new approach to measuring organizational performance are concepts such as the following:

- Fewer is better: Concentrate on measuring the vital few key variables rather than the trivial many.

- Measures should be linked to the factors needed for success: key business drivers.

- Measures should be a mix of past, present, and future to ensure that the organization is concerned with all three perspectives.

- Measures should be based around the needs of customers, shareholders, and other key stakeholders.

- Measures should start at the top and flow down to all levels of employees in the organization.

- Multiple indices can be combined into a single index to give a better overall assessment of performance.

- Measures should be changed or at least adjusted as the environment and your strategy changes.

- Measures need to have targets or goals established that are based on research rather than arbitrary numbers.

CHARACTERISTICS OF AN EFFECTIVE MEASUREMENT SYSTEM

Vital Few Versus Trivial Many

The maximum number of metrics any organization should have as overall measures is 20. No one individual can monitor and control more than 20 variables on a regular basis. The key to having a successful set of metrics is paring down your database to the vital few key metrics that are linked to your success. Large high-tech organizations tend to resist the concept that a complicated organization can be measured using 20 or less metrics. Pointing out that large high-tech companies like AT&T manage to perform fairly well with four key metrics is somewhat misleading. AT&T may have four overall metrics, but thousands of individual metrics are collected, reported, and summarized into aggregate statistics that are indices of overall performance. For example, EVA, or economic value-added, may be the only overall financial metric that AT&T concentrates on, but it consists of a variety of subsidiary metrics. It is alright to have hundreds or even thousands of metrics in your organization's database. It is just that no individual should have to focus on more than a few major ones. It helps to think of your measurement scorecard like a dashboard on a car, which has a few key gauges that need to be monitored fairly regularly, a few that need to be looked at with less frequency, and some warning lights that alert us to possible problems. The metrics that are not key to your company's success can be looked at as the warning lights. These are important, but they may not need to be monitored every day or reviewed in meetings every month.

For example, I was recently working with a manufacturing company that was having trouble with the idea that safety not be one of its key metrics. The company had an excellent prevention-based approach to safety that had resulted in a safety record that was among the best in its business. It agreed to keep safety metrics in the scorecard, but make it a subsidiary measure because of its long track record of success in this area. Safety for the company was making sure there is enough oil in your car. Not having enough oil can certainly cause some major problems, but if you drive a new car and change the oil every 2,000 miles, you don't need to spend much time watching the oil gauge as you drive.

Linkage to Vision, Values, and Key Success Factors

Along with having a reasonable number of metrics, another key to success is to select measures that are linked to your key success factors. For example, if you have identified the technical competence of your people as being something that gives you an edge on your competition, you'd better make sure that you have a measure of technical competence in your scorecard. Similarly, if one of your key success factors is your marketing ability, a metric is needed that measures the effectiveness of your marketing efforts. If you are serious about running your organization with a specific set of values, it is also important that you have metrics in your scorecard that tell you how well you live by your professed values. For example, one of the stated values of Ciba-Geigy is to become known as a benchmark in the areas of safety and environmental protection. To achieve this vision, the company has some very good metrics in their scorecard, along with comparisons to others in the industry, so it can tell how close its own performance levels are to other companies viewed as world-class in these areas.

Metrics Should Focus on the Past, Present, and Future

The problem with most measures is that they focus on the past. How much money did we make last quarter, how many accidents did we have this month, and how many units did we ship? Measuring the most recent period's performance is critical for any organization. However, if this is all you measure, you may not be around in the next 5 years. Past and present metrics are the easiest to come up with, because we typically have data on these types of metrics, and these results have actually happened. You don't need to do any projections to find out how much money was made last month; you can look at the actual figures. Future measures help predict success over a longer term than next month or next quarter. An example of a future-oriented metric for an engineering and construction firm might be the dollar values of outstanding proposals. Locked-in future orders might be a future-oriented metric for a manufacturing company. Dollars in sales from new products might be a good present and future-oriented metric for a company looking to expand its sales by focusing on the development of more new products.

Metrics Should Be Linked to the Needs of Customers, Shareholders, and Employees

Selecting the right metrics or measures is actually much more than deciding what to measure. It is, in fact, a key part of your overall strategy for success. Select the wrong performance metrics and you may go out of business although all graphs indicate that you are healthy. Select the wrong metrics and your worst nightmare might come true—employees might actually perform according to these metrics. The concepts in this book are quite simple. It is almost common sense that all organizations need a balanced scorecard and that fewer measures are better than too many. However, coming up with a good precise set of metrics that actually predicts your success is quite difficult. Doing so often requires expensive research and some trial and error to settle on just the right index or metric that predicts your success in the marketplace. For a while, many companies thought that if you focused on quality, everything else would take care of itself. Profits would roll in from customers who were delighted with the quality of your products and services. Over the years, we learned that focusing on quality is not the answer. Companies went out of business with the best quality in their industries. A more recent hot button in the field of corporate measurement is economic value-added (EVA) as the magic financial index that will lead you to financial success. EVA is discussed in Chapter 5, but remember that no single statistic is going to transform any organization. EVA is proving to be a excellent overall index of financial performance that seems to drive the right behavior and builds shareholder value. However, if this is the only metric in your scorecard, you're in trouble.

The key to an effective set of metrics is to have many of them, not one important one. Success is about balance, not a mindless focus on quality, shareholder value, profit, or any other individual measure.

Metrics Should Flow Down to All Levels and Should Be Consistent

Many organizations today have developed a balanced set of metrics for evaluating their overall performance. The problem is that individual business units, locations, and functions often have sets of measures that are completely unrelated to the overall corporate metrics. Objectives are set and measures are identified for things that are easy to count and achieve, but often have nothing to do with the organization's overall success. Metrics need to be defined for the highest level of the organization first and then flow down to all levels and functions. Metrics at one level should lead to metrics at the next higher level, and so forth. Defining performance measures in this manner ensures that you do not have any disconnects or inconsistencies in how or what you measure.

Multiple Measures Can Be Combined into Several Overall Indices of Performance

A number of organizations struggle with the concept that it is possible to measure performance by looking at a dozen or so metrics. One aerospace company reengineered its measurement system and reduced the number of metrics at the highest level from more than 200 to 64 key result indicators. Sixty-four is obviously too many metrics for any organization, but it was not willing to give up any of these important measures. One way of reducing the number of measures to a reasonable number is to assign a weight to each individual measure in a family of metrics and develop an index that is an aggregate statistic. For example, one organization collected data on a number of individual metrics relating to employee well-being and satisfaction:

- Employee morale survey.
- Focus groups.
- Absenteeism.
- Hours worked per week.
- Turnover.
- Grievances/complaints.
- Requests for transfer (in and out of departments).

Each of these metrics is weighted on the basis of its importance and an overall employee satisfaction index (ESI) is computed once every 6 months. Seven individual measures thereby have been reduced to one.

Monitoring the overall ESI levels and trends saves time, and the backup data are still in the database if an individual needs to see them. Combining multiple metrics into a single index is an excellent way of aggregating and simplifying performance reporting. This practice of aggregating data into a single statistic is risky, however, because the aggregate statistic often hides trends that might be noticed in the subsidiary measures. I recommend piloting aggregate statistics in small areas of the business to see if you have summarized the data too far. The desire for simplicity in your database is often achieved at the expense of the amount of detail in the data you collect. Although it is much easier to look at an overall safety index than to review 14 individual measures of safety, the safety index might not move much unless there are drastic changes in performance. Hence, problems might not be noticed until they become very serious. The logic for the idea that a few key metrics is better than 50 good ones is based on the idea that no one individual can regularly monitor, control, and focus on 50 variables. Mentally, all managers who receive 50 charts a week pull out those that they think are most important and focus most of their attention on them.

Metrics Should Be Changed as Your Strategy and Situation Changes

Sometimes a company will begin collecting data on a specific metric because it has been found to be a problem. For example, a major corporation spent 3 years tracking the percentage of meetings that start on time. This usually would not be important enough to include in the CEO's overall scorecard, but he was concerned with it. The company had a culture where people always seemed to be late to meetings; someone determined how many hundreds of thousands of dollars this was costing the company in lost productivity per year; it got the CEO's attention. After a couple of years, people showed improvement and stopped showing up late to meetings, so the measure was dropped from the scorecard.

Several years ago, a major computer manufacturer received some clear feedback from customers that had to do with its responsiveness to customers' needs and concerns. After conducting a number of focus groups to find out what types of things the employees did that made them seem unresponsive, it often boiled down to things like returning phone messages and talking to a person versus voice mail when calling an employee. To fix this problem, the company did a massive training effort that taught all employees certain standards for telephone service. For example, your message on your voice mail had to be changed daily, you had to announce where you would be, and you had to leave an alternative number so the caller could reach you or another individual. The company conducted telephone service audits using the mystery shopper approach; it put together a telephone service index that gave scores based on overall performance. Telephone service scores became one of the major measures in executive scorecards for a while, until the problem decreased. It has now dropped the measure because the index showed that performance improved greatly and maintained high levels for a long enough period of time for the company to feel comfortable.

Metrics are added and deleted from your scorecard as needs dictate. Customers' need for changes in the marketplace often dictate adding new metrics and dropping old ones. Competitive pricing never was a concern for Giorgio Armani back in the 1980s and early 1990s. In 1 year, the price of an Armani suit increased about 15 to 20 percent and no one batted an eyelash. Men with lots of money, or those conscious of their image, thought nothing of shelling out up to $2,000 for an Armani "black label" suit. In the 1990s, however, even Armani found that it had to be concerned with competitive pricing. That same guy who paid $2,000 for his suits 5 years ago, now buys many of his clothes from the Gap and is more concerned with value than with status.

Metrics Need to Have Targets or Goals Based on Research

A graph of a measure without knowing the target or goal is meaningless data that does not help manage performance. You have to know what is good, how good is the best, and so on. Goal or objective setting has been done in most organizations since the 1970s when George Odiorne introduced us to management by objectives (MBO). The problem in many organizations is that targets or goals are set in a completely arbitrary fashion, based on history. We look at how we did last year and bump it up by 10 percent, or if we're into challenge or stretch goals, we make up a ridiculous goal like "tenfold improvement," thinking it will cause employees to stretch and find different ways of completing work processes. Arbitrary goals are stupid. Goals are designed to give us a target to shoot for that is challenging, worthwhile, and achievable. Goals need to be based on research about what key competitors are doing and on a study of benchmark companies that are perhaps outside of the industry.

For example, Northrop Grumman, the aerospace firm, collected some data about seven years ago on how many days it took to issue a purchase order. The cycle time was 40 days. It did some research at other aerospace companies and found that the best purchase order cycle in an aerospace firm took only 10 days. Not content to be the best of the worst, the company did some benchmarking and found a company of the same size that managed to issue a purchase order in just two days. Two days became the long-term stretch goal for Northrop Grumman, which is a long way from where it started, 40 days, but it was a good stretch goal because it was based on research. The goal has worked very well. As of this writing, it is down from 40 days to about four days, well on the way to reaching the stretch goal.

Arbitrary goals are quite easy to spot because they are most always even or round numbers like 10 or 98 percent. This is an unsophisticated approach to goal setting that shows that the organization is not willing to spend the time to set goals based on research rather than numbers pulled out of the air. The real danger in setting an arbitrary goal is that employees might achieve it and cause a major problem. Achieving an arbitrary goal on one metric may cause severe problems in other areas of the organization. Another, less severe problem is that employees will not support stretch goals if they believe that they are based on arbitrary numbers. Setting goals based on research seems like common sense, but there are many arbitrary goals in most major corporations and government organizations I have consulted. More on this in Chapter 14, which discusses how to set good targets or goals for the measures in your scorecard.

STRATEGIC MEASUREMENT MODEL

Measurement is easy. What is difficult is measuring the right things and learning to ignore other interesting data that do not help you become more successful. This book links measures to what is critical for the success of your organization. As you can see in the model in Figure 1.1, you begin by defining what your organization does and your vision for the future. Next, an organization should identify the key success factors it needs to concentrate on to differentiate itself from competitors. During this phase, the organization also identifies important business fundamentals on which it must focus to maintain its success. Business fundamentals tend to be issues that all organizations in the industry need to concen-

FIGURE 1.1 Strategic Measurement Model

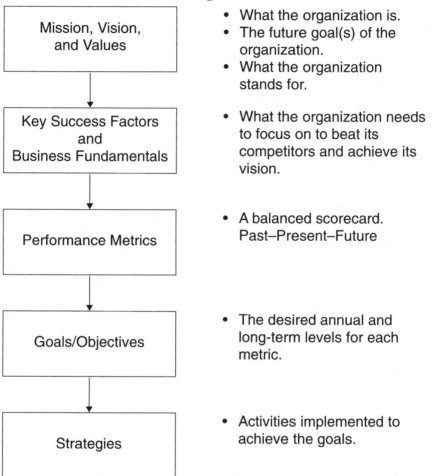

Mission, Vision, and Values	• What the organization is. • The future goal(s) of the organization. • What the organization stands for.
Key Success Factors and Business Fundamentals	• What the organization needs to focus on to beat its competitors and achieve its vision.
Performance Metrics	• A balanced scorecard. Past–Present–Future
Goals/Objectives	• The desired annual and long-term levels for each metric.
Strategies	• Activities implemented to achieve the goals.

trate on, such as profitability, growth, or regulation. Selecting the key success factors for your organization is a major part of a business strategy, because you have selected the areas of performance on which you will concentrate. These could be strengths you will continue to exploit or weaknesses that need to be corrected. From the key success factors and business fundamentals come the measures, or metrics. Once the organization has defined all of the important measures on its scorecard, specific goals or objectives need to be set for each metric. Goals are based upon research and should help the organization to achieve its overall vision. Care must be taken to make sure that all the goals link up well with each other, so that improved performance on one measure does not cause deterioration of performance on another measure. Once the goals or objectives have been identified, strategies or action plans need to be identified that will allow you to achieve them.

NO MAGIC BULLET

Redesigning your measurement system is not something that will ensure a successful organization. This is not another management fad. Serious management practices such as reengineering and TQM (Total Quality Management) never live up to their promises as revolutionary new ways of doing business when treated as a fad. Coming up with a good solid set of metrics and actually using it to manage will save thousands of hours of time wasted reviewing charts and graphs in meetings and reading reports on statistics that do not really matter. All organizations measure something. Large organizations tend to measure and report on just about everything that might be measurable or somewhat important. Armies of employees do nothing but collect, summarize, and report data. Armies of managers and technical professionals spend time reviewing these data and attempting to pull out something meaningful from the mass of charts they receive each week. Small organizations tend not to waste time measuring frivolous things and concentrate only on a few key metrics like sales, yield, profits, and productivity. The scorecards in these organizations are just as bad because all of their measures are focused on the past and do nothing to help predict future success.

Benefits of Implementing Strategic Measurement

The most common objection to any effort like reengineering your measurement system is a lack of time. Clients often suggest that they are too busy making money to take time out for an overhead-draining activity like this. If times are good, there is never time for this, and if times are bad, the motivation to fix your measurement system is even lower. "We need to get some new work in here, or work on salvaging a relationship with a major customer—we don't have time for a long-term project like this that may take six months or longer." Although many of the benefits of an improved scorecard or set of metrics will not be realized until later years, there are a number of immediate benefits. Some of these benefits include the following:

- An 80 percent reduction in the volume of reports that were generated on a monthly basis by a corporate finance function

- A more than 50 percent reduction in the amount of time spent in monthly senior management meetings

- A 60 percent reduction in the pounds of reports that were printed each day, reporting performance data

- An increased ability to focus on both the long- and short-term success of the organization

- A better balance between meeting the needs of customers, shareholders, and employees

- The elimination of up to an hour each day spent by managers reviewing and attempting to interpret unimportant performance data

- A way to make the vision and values real to employees and to track progress toward achieving the vision and living the values

This is, indeed, quite a bit of work. However, the time you invest up front to eliminate the unnecessary data from your databases will continue to pay off for years. Business is just not all that complicated. Taking care of your customers, shareholders, employees, and suppliers will make you successful. Many of the most successful organizations focus on only a few key metrics. For Federal Express, everything centers around people (employees), service (customers), and profits (shareholders). Every employee from the CEO to the package sorter attempts to achieve a balance in meeting the needs of these three groups. AT&T focuses on a few key measures that relate to adding value for shareholders (economic value-added), employees (people value-added), and customers (customer value-added). Throughout big organizations like AT&T and Federal Express there are thousands of metrics, but all of them fall within the major categories outlined, and no one individual needs to look at more than a few for his or her job.

Problems with
Most Measurement
Systems

HAYSTACKS

Data, like hay, is usually dry
And piled in stacks and measured by the bit.
And how like the needle information is: it
Always has a point and it needs an eye.

—Thomas F. Gilbert

Why is it that some organizations work with such precision that they measure defects per million products or opportunities? How is it that airlines fly thousands of flights per day from airports all over the world and have less than one serious accident for every million flights? Yet, if you take your car in to be repaired or have someone fix your copy machine, the technician fixes it right the first time about 60 percent of the time. Flying a 747 is certainly more difficult than doing a tune-up on a Chevrolet. Some of the reasons for these discrepancies in quality level have to do with training, workload, and quality control techniques. A lot of it has to do with data though. Airline pilots spend the majority of their time monitoring key measures and controlling the plane so that it safely arrives at the right destination almost every single time. Pilots have good data. They understand the relationships between different measures and they know how to adjust various aspects of the plane's controls based upon the data. Managers and professionals in many organizations today are like a pilot trying to fly a plane with only half the instruments needed and a bunch of additional instruments that measure irrelevant data. With the confusing array of data that most managers have, it's no wonder that so many problems occur in so many of the places where we work.

Practically every organization has some type of problem with its measurement system. Some need only a minor tune-up, whereas others need a major overhaul. In this chapter, we'll examine some of the most typical problems that occur in an organization's approach to measuring performance.

TOO MUCH DATA

I once worked with a major telecommunications company that had 106 individual databases. Each database contained between 75 and 100 metrics or measures of performance. Every month, the company collected and reported between 7,500 and 10,000 measures. Now, a single individual reviews far less data than that, but many of the managers I talked to said that they commonly review 100 to 200 pages of data every week. When I asked managers how much of the data received was actually used, most said, "About 5%."

Having too much data is the most common and most serious problem an organization can have with its measurement system. The reason is that it wastes a great deal of valuable time. Managers have to weed through mounds of irrelevant data to get to the few buried kernels that they really need to manage their functions. A second and more serious problem is that the data they pay attention to and use are often the wrong data. The metrics they use are selected because of superstition. In other words, managers think that a particular measure is related to success, when there is little hard evidence that this is the case.

So, how do you know if you have too much data? As a general rule, no individual employee should have to monitor more than 15 to 20 measures. If you are the CEO of a major corporation, 15 to 20 measures is a reasonable number of variables to manage. If you manage a department, facility, or business unit, a smaller number of measures is appropriate. A good number to shoot for is about a dozen, with half of those measures being the most important. This rule of no more than a dozen measures applies to everyone from senior managers to the mail room staff.

ALL MEASURES ARE SHORT-TERM FOCUSED

Many small and medium-sized organizations do not collect too much data. They do not have time to waste collecting and reporting data that are not really needed to run the business. They have a different type of problem. The only types of data they collect are financial and operational data. Go into your typical restaurant, medical clinic, or any small-to-medium-sized organization, and you will find all sorts of financial and operational statistics. The organization can tell you its overhead expense, income, profit, and any other figure from the general ledger. It can also tell you how many customers are processed per day or how many units are shipped, what the scrap rate is, and the productivity levels of the employees. These are all important measures in running an organization, but they are all short-term and focus on how we did today, this month, or this quarter.

Focusing only on the short term is one of the reasons that American organizations struggle to survive over the long haul. Wall Street encourages short-term measurement and short-term thinking because it does not trust longer-term measures such as investment in R&D and measures of customer satisfaction. The financial community rewards companies for laying off employees, or "downsizing," with higher stock prices. These organizations often do well for a year or two, but end up failing in the long run because all those smart people that they laid off or eliminated through early retirements are what gave them their competitive edge.

Longer-term measures that any organization must record include the following:

- Customer satisfaction.

- Employee satisfaction.

- Product/service quality.

- Public responsibility measures.

Happier employees or happier customers may not result in an immediate financial benefit, but they are what's going to keep you in business 5 or 10 years from now. Some companies believe that happier customers and happier employees lead to short-term results as well. One large organization recently began basing about one-third of compensation for key executives and managers on the levels of customer satisfaction that their organizations achieve.

LACK OF DETAIL

Sometimes the data that are collected and reported are summarized so much as to make the information meaningless. Steve just got promoted to Regional Sales Manager for a large pharmaceutical firm. One of his ma-

TABLE 2.1   Sample Expense Report

Item	June	YTD	Last Year
Proposal costs	$48,000	$152,300	$34,500
Inside labor (sales)	$8,400	$36,000	$4,900
Inside labor (support)	$12,600	$43,800	$6,300
Word processing	$3,400	$18,200	$4,100
Graphics	$16,400	$21,300	$9,300
Miscellaneous	$7,200	$33,000	$9,900
Travel and Entertainment	$48,700	$272,000	$41,100
Airlines	$18,400	$97,000	$16,200
Hotel	$8,200	$51,400	$4,700
Car rental	$9,300	$46,000	$8,700
Food & miscellaneous	$12,800	$77,600	$11,500
Telephone	$11,200	$56,000	$3,900
Samples	$19,400	$88,000	$17,400

jor responsibilities is controlling expenses. He knows from being a salesman himself that expenses can get out of hand. Salespeople are not given
a set budget, but expected to use their good judgment in deciding how to
spend money trying to land or keep a customer. The report Steve received
every month looked like the one in Table 2.1.

Once a month, Steve had a meeting with his sales managers and reviewed the monthly expense statements. He was getting heat from his
boss because proposal costs were up by about 40 percent from last June
and sales were only up by 6 percent from last June. Telephone costs were
up by almost three times what they were last year and Steve read his team
the riot act about this. When he talked to his team about the telephone expense, the team members all pointed their fingers at each other, claiming
that their own people were surely not responsible for the increase. Frustrated, Steve called the corporate sales office and asked for a breakdown
of telephone expense by state, by city, and by individual salesperson so
he could find the abusers. Corporate sales informed him that the data
were entered each month and the only breakdown he could get was by
state. In analyzing the data on a state-by-state basis, no trends were ap-
parent—they all had shown a significant increase in telephone expense.

Steve ended up very frustrated because he could not tell who was responsible for the huge increases in proposal costs and phone bills. The information he received was not sufficiently detailed to use in controlling expenses, which is a fairly common problem in organizations. A report like the one Steve received is useless as a tool for controlling expenses. Looking at how much money was spent after the fact does not provide enough information to use in doing a better job of controlling expenses. If a budget had been established for each line item and deviation from budget was shown, this would not have added much value. Without the detail, Steve would be unable still to determine the individual or area responsible for overspending.

MEASURES THAT DRIVE THE WRONG PERFORMANCE

Measuring professionals like scientists, engineers, attorneys, and accountants is tough. Intellectual work is difficult to measure objectively, so organizations look for factors that can be counted and measured objectively—measuring things that can be counted may not be what is really important. Meaningful outputs for professionals include ideas, information, and problems avoided. These outputs are very difficult to measure.

Ten Pages Per Day

I worked for a company that developed customized training programs for corporate clients. One of the measures for the writers, or "instructional developers," was the number of pages they wrote per day. The standard was that each writer ought to average 10 pages a day. Employees' performance was measured every week against this standard, and for the most part it was met. The quality of those 10 pages varied dramatically, however. Some writers would produce 10 pages of accurate, well-written instruction. Others turned out 10 pages of garbage. Quality was in the eye of the beholder. If you worked on a project for Hal, you knew that he would rip apart your writing and make you rewrite it three or four times before he accepted it. If you got lucky to work on a project for Ray, however, you could turn in 10 pages of trash. If it was neatly typed and contained no glaring errors, it was fine for Ray. How many pages a writer writes per day is easy to measure objectively, but it is not what is really important. How many good pages are written per day is what is impor-

TABLE 2.2   University Tenure Point System

Publication of a book

Single author, major publisher	50 points
1/2 authorship, academic publisher	35 points
3 to 4 authors, academic publisher	25 points
Book chapter	10 points

Journal articles

Single author, class A journal	25 points
Multiple authors, class A journal	15 points
Single author, class B journal	10 points
Multiple authors, class B journal	8 points

Conference presentations*

Keynote address, international	25 points
Keynote address, national	22 points
Invited presentation, international	20 points
Invited presentation, national	18 points
Unsolicited presentations (national conferences)	10–20 points
Local presentations	5 points

*50 percent of points are earned when there are multiple presenters.

tant; there is no one definition of goodness. The quality of writing is something that must be judged subjectively.

Publications and Speeches

Many research-and-development facilities and most universities measure scientists and professors on how many publications they author and how many papers they present at technical conferences. One university had a point system with which professors were judged in their journey toward receiving tenure (see Table 2.2).

Actually, the university that has this published point system was considered leading edge because it at least published some of the criteria for earning tenure and measured performance objectively. A research-and-development function in a major corporation employs a similar point system for evaluating its researchers. If you were the internal customers of an R&D facility, or if you were a university student, would you really care how many papers your researchers or professors publish? I doubt it. Measures like this drive the wrong performance. The scientists at this R&D facility knew how to play the game, just as university professors have learned how to play the tenure game. One of the R&D scientists explained it well:

> The system works pretty well once you know how to get points. You see, if you come up with a good journal article you get points for that. Then you present the material at a local meeting of a national conference, get it published as a chapter in a book a colleague of yours is editing, and you end up getting credit about five times for the same piece of work. Some of the research that gets published and presented at conferences is of absolutely no value. Someone shows a correlation between two variables where the correlation is already well understood, or something like that, and ends up getting 150 points for it.

The purpose of an R&D facility is not to publish articles and make presentations. This measure is of little value because it is not really related to why the organization exists in the first place: to develop new technologies that lead to new products and to allow for enhancements to existing products and processes.

Chicken Efficiency

Most organizations have one or two key measures that are considered far more important than others. They are often called management hot buttons. Sometimes they are profits, sales, or units shipped. For example, at a fast-food chain that specializes in chicken, it's "chicken efficiency." Every restaurant manager and employee knows that chicken efficiency is the most important of all measures. Managers put together graphs to illustrate their chicken efficiency levels to their bosses each month.

Chicken efficiency is a scrap measure. It is a ratio of how many pieces of chicken are sold to how many are thrown away. This fast-food chain has very strict quality standards on how long the chicken can sit under the heat lamps before it has to be thrown away. What performance is this chicken efficiency measure going to drive? A manager explained it this way:

If I want to look good on my chicken efficiency numbers, all I have to do is one thing: don't cook any chicken. If I cook it and I don't sell it, I might have to throw it away, which messes up my chicken efficiency numbers. If I don't cook it, the customer has to wait about 20 minutes, but very few get mad enough to leave without their chicken.

Here is the scenario that results from this procedure: A customer enters this establishment and orders a couple of chickens. Most likely, they won't be ready and he will have to wait. He might get angry and never return to this establishment even though he loves its chicken. Although the company has effective measures of chicken efficiency, it does not have a method for measuring lost customers. The point is that the chicken efficiency measure drives performances that causes dissatisfied customers. By selecting the wrong measure on which to focus, the company promotes poor service to its companies.

MEASURES OF COURTESY VERSUS COMPETENCE

A related type of problem is organizations that choose to focus on measures of courtesy versus competence. We encounter this all the time in service organizations. For example, an airline's schedules are always delayed, but the flight attendants always remember to stand by the door and smile and say "good-bye" to us as passengers walk off the plane an hour late again.

Examples of nice but incompetent people can be found in every profession. Sometimes the things that organizations choose to measure drive this nice but incompetent performance. A supermarket in Detroit measured its checkout clerks on whether they told customers to "Have a nice day" as they handed the customers their receipts. They even put in an incentive program to encourage clerks to tell every customers to have a nice day. They kept this up until they did a little research that told them that over half the customers didn't even notice whether or not they were told to have a nice day; many of the other customers said they hated hearing the phrase.

Nordstrom, believed to be the department store with the highest caliber of service, does not measure smiles or how quickly the salespersons greet customers, or what they say. Rather than training its people to be service robots, it encourages each individual to use a style they are comfortable with in dealing with customers. However, Nordstrom's most-important measure is sales. If you work at Nordstrom and you do not sell, you're gone, no matter how nice you are to customers. Nordstrom does focus on courtesy and does train its employees, but it measures them on what really matters: sales and repeat business from the same customers.

MEASURES OF BEHAVIOR VERSUS ACCOMPLISHMENTS

Quality gurus will tell you that if you want to get good quality every single time in your products or services, you need to control your processes and not focus on inspecting the product or the service. A preventive approach to quality involves controlling process variables that have an impact on product or service characteristics. In many organizations (both manufacturing and service), processes are performed by people, not machines. This means that to control processes, you have to control behavior. Logic says that if everyone follows a prescribed path of behaviors, predictable results will occur most of the time. Behavioral measures are measures of what people do. Accomplishment measures are measures of meaningful performance. For example, some behavioral and accomplishment measures for an automotive service technician are shown in Table 2.3.

The problem with measuring behavior is that often the behaviors being asked for do not ensure that the quality of the service or product is good. The danger in measuring behavior rather than accomplishments is illustrated by the case of two salespeople: Lynn and Larry. Lynn and Larry had both worked for Eddie for several years. Recently, Eddie had spent some time at Xerox and IBM to learn about their scientific approaches to selling. Both companies believe that selling is a process—a process that can be broken down into its component behaviors. In fact, Xerox had done quite a bit of research to identify the specific sequence of

TABLE 2.3   Automotive Service Technician Measures

Behavior Measures	Accomplishment Measures
Uses diagnostic software support.	Percent service comebacks (problems not fixed right the first time).
Follows all safety guidelines.	Labor cost versus standard.
Uses correct parts and tools.	Work orders/day (productivity measure).

behaviors that are highly correlated with exceptional sales results. IBM also believes that effective selling is a science, not an art. If you can identify the critical behaviors and teach everyone to perform those behaviors, sales will naturally increase.

Based on his research at IBM and Xerox, Eddie defined the selling process for his own company as consisting of the following phases:

    I. Generate leads

   II. Qualify leads

  III. Build relationship

  IV. Submit proposal

   V. Account growth

Working with his salespeople, Eddie identified specific behaviors involved in each of the five phases of the sales cycle and developed measures for the important behaviors. Salespeople initially rebelled against all of this measurement, but eventually became used to it. Everyone, that is, except Lynn. She had always been a nonconformist. Lynn was abrasive, frequently missed sales meetings, and was generally not well liked. Larry, on the other hand was a "team player." Everyone loved working with him. He was always in a good mood, told some great stories and jokes, and knew more about the company's products than many of the technical support experts.

As a pilot test, Eddie decided to introduce his behavior or process measures while he continued to track the old accomplishment-based measures. Table 2.4 is a summary of the behavior and accomplishment measures and how Lynn and Larry compared during the first two quarters of the year.

Larry looks great on all of the behavioral measures. His performance is almost always at or above the goal, and looks fantastic compared to Lynn's. Larry's performance is often three or four times better. He's also been working a lot of hours the last 6 months to look good on these new behavioral measures. Lynn has done her best to ignore these new measures, and rarely even works 8 hours a day. Her behavioral measures indicate that she generates only a few leads, responds to only a few requests for proposals (RFPs), and does not spend a lot of time bonding with her

TABLE 2.4   Behavior and Accomplishment Measures, January–June

Behavior Measures	Lynn	Larry	Goal
Number of contact/lead sheets completed	2	62	40
Percent of leads qualified	100	48	50
Number of personal meetings with leads per month (average)	1	14	12
Number of RFPs/RFQs received	6	18	12
Number of proposals submitted	2	18	6
Number of additional opportunities identified in new accounts/customers	4	11	6
Number of relationship-building activities with key decision makers	6	31	24
Hours worked per week	36	64	50
Accomplishment Measures			
Proposal win ratio	100%	22%	50%
Dollar value of won proposals	$2,850,000	$640,000	$1 Million
Billing per month	$320,000	$111,000	$250,000
Gross margin per project	61%	37%	40%

clients at dinners and sporting events. How she achieves the results she does is a great mystery to both Larry and his boss Eddie.

Lynn and Larry's story illustrates the fallacy of concentrating on behavioral measures. No one would argue that the behaviors being measured (generating leads and preparing proposals) are important to the sales process. However, if you stress behavior rather than accomplishments, you will likely get performance like Larry's.

MEASURES ENCOURAGE COMPETITION AND DISCOURAGE TEAMWORK

Sometimes you'd think that business units within the same company actually compete with each other by the way they are out for themselves and refuse to share with some of their sister organizations. Measures that organizations select often encourage this competitiveness. Reports often compare one business unit with another's performance, rather than comparing each to its own performance and goals. This is a subtle form of discouraging teamwork. Whoever is number one likes being there and does not want to share secrets with the other business units or locations.

Most performance appraisal systems also include measures that promote competition and discourage teams of employees to work together. Individuals are assessed, not teams in most systems. Individuals also get promotions and raises, not teams. Focusing exclusively on measures of individual performance is a common but detrimental practice in an organization that is attempting to foster a spirit of cooperation and sharing. In these days, when downsizing is one of the favored corporate strategies for profit improvement, many organizations require each manager to rank her staff from best to worst after evaluating each one's performance. This is done so that if a layoff is necessary, the manager will know which employees will be selected. The biggest danger comes in telling employees where they stand relative to their peers. Whether you are number one or number fifteen, learning how you rank against others is devastating to teamwork.

Evaluating Your Existing Measurement System

Measurement is boring. Collecting numbers and looking at charts and graphs of those numbers are not exciting for most of us. For many people, measurement is nothing more than busywork.

Implementing a change effort to make your organization more customer-focused does not necessarily entail more measurements. Organizations have always spent a large portion of time measuring and reporting data. Those that follow the Baldrige Award criteria as a roadmap for improving their organizations have learned that selecting the vital few metrics on which to collect data is what is important, rather than collecting statistics on everything. It is also important to have what Robert Kaplan and David Norton refer to as the "balanced scorecard." In "Putting the Balanced Scorecard to Work" (*Harvard Business Review,* September/October 1993), the authors suggest that most organizations do not have a balanced set of measures. They concentrate almost exclusively on short-term financial measures and ignore longer-term, more strategic measures such as customer satisfaction, employee satisfaction, and growth.

According to Section 2.0 of the Baldrige Award criteria, a balanced set of metrics for any organization should include roughly the same amount of data in each of the following boxes:

- Customer satisfaction.

- Employee satisfaction.

- Financial performance.

- Operational performance (for example, cycle time, productivity, and so on).

- Product/service quality.

- Supplier performance.

- Safety/environmental/public responsibility.

In most organizations, about 80 percent of the data they collect fall into two boxes: financial and operational. Once a year, they perform a customer satisfaction survey, and once every 3 years, they perform an employee morale survey. They have a few statistics on product quality and safety, and inspect incoming supplier shipments. This is just what we mean by not having a balanced scorecard. For most organizations, almost all of their data are in two of the seven boxes. This is a short-sighted way to measure an organization's performance because it focuses only on measures that impact the organization today. The survey in this chapter will evaluate, among other things, whether your organization has a balanced set of measures. It will also look at how you use data on those measures to improve performance.

Although measurement is critical to improved performance, organizations do not always get what they measure. If measurement by itself really had that much impact on behavior, anyone who had a scale would never be overweight. So, although having a good balanced set of measures does not guarantee success by itself, selecting the wrong measures surely leads to disaster. Measurement only provides you with data. If the data are not used to make good business decisions and to drive improvement efforts, a good measurement system is of little value.

This survey allows you to evaluate the measures and measurement system used in your own organization. By completing this self-assessment instrument, you will learn the characteristics of an effective measurement system and how well yours stands up to these standards and practices.

QUESTIONNAIRE DIRECTIONS

The questionnaire is divided into three parts, each addressing some aspect of your measurement system. Part I (questions 1 to 5) is about your overall approach to measurement. Part II (questions 6 to 40) asks about specific types of measures. Part III (questions 41 to 50) is about how to analyze and use the data to improve your organization. Read each statement and check the appropriate box, depending on the extent to which you strongly agree (5) or strongly disagree (1) with the statement. Answer every question even if you have to guess. The scope of the questionnaire should pertain to your entire organization or at least a sufficiently large portion of the company or organization that could be a stand-alone business/organization. For example, you could do a business unit rather than the whole company, or one hospital in a chain of hospitals. You could and should not use the questionnaire to apply to a single department such as radiology or human resources.

MEASUREMENT SYSTEM SELF-ASSESSMENT

Part I: Overall Approach to Measurement

1. The metrics in our database are tightly linked to the key success factors that will allow us to differentiate ourselves from our competitors.

   (5) Strongly Agree   (4) Agree   (3) Somewhat Agree   (2) Disagree   (1) Strongly Disagree

2. Our database was built with a plan, rather than being something that just evolved over time.

   (5) Strongly Agree   (4) Agree   (3) Somewhat Agree   (2) Disagree   (1) Strongly Disagree

3. Our CEO or President looks at no more than 20 measures every month to evaluate the overall organization's performance.

   (5) Strongly Agree   (4) Agree   (3) Somewhat Agree   (2) Disagree   (1) Strongly Disagree

4. Measures of performance are mostly consistent across our business units/locations.

   (5) Strongly Agree   (4) Agree   (3) Somewhat Agree   (2) Disagree   (1) Strongly Disagree

5. We have a well-balanced set of measures, with about equal amounts of measures/data in each of the following categories: financial performance, operational performance, customer satisfaction, employee satisfaction, product/service quality, supplier performance, and safety/environmental performance.

   (5) Strongly Agree   (4) Agree   (3) Somewhat Agree   (2) Disagree   (1) Strongly Disagree

Part II: Specific Types of Measures on Your Scorecard

Customer-Related Measures

6. Our database includes good hard measures of customer satisfaction/ value such as repeat/lost business, returns, and so on.

    (5) Strongly Agree   (4) Agree   (3) Somewhat Agree   (2) Disagree   (1) Strongly Disagree

7. Our organization collects data on both customer satisfaction and perceived value levels using a variety of techniques such as telephone surveys, mail surveys, and focus groups.

    (5) Strongly Agree   (4) Agree   (3) Somewhat Agree   (2) Disagree   (1) Strongly Disagree

8. Our surveys for measuring customer satisfaction focus on delighting customers rather than just satisfying them.

    (5) Strongly Agree   (4) Agree   (3) Somewhat Agree   (2) Disagree   (1) Strongly Disagree

9. What we ask customers in our satisfaction surveys or discussions is based upon thorough research to identify customers' most important requirements.

    (5) Strongly Agree   (4) Agree   (3) Somewhat Agree   (2) Disagree   (1) Strongly Disagree

10. We combine various hard and soft measures of customer satisfaction and value into an overall customer satisfaction index.

    (5) Strongly Agree   (4) Agree   (3) Somewhat Agree   (2) Disagree   (1) Strongly Disagree

Employee-Related Measures

11. We survey our employees at least once a year to determine their satisfaction levels with various aspects of how the organization is run.

    (5) Strongly Agree   (4) Agree   (3) Somewhat Agree   (2) Disagree   (1) Strongly Disagree

12. Employee surveys are anonymous and more than 75 percent are returned each year.

    (5) Strongly Agree   (4) Agree   (3) Somewhat Agree   (2) Disagree   (1) Strongly Disagree

13. Research is done to determine what is important to employees before putting together or buying a survey with standard questions.

    (5) Strongly Agree   (4) Agree   (3) Somewhat Agree   (2) Disagree   (1) Strongly Disagree

14. Our organization collects data on other metrics that relate to employee satisfaction such as voluntary turnover, absenteeism, hours worked per week, requests for transfers, stress-related illness, and so on.

    (5) Strongly Agree   (4) Agree   (3) Somewhat Agree   (2) Disagree   (1) Strongly Disagree

15. Individual measures of employee satisfaction are aggregated into an overall employee satisfaction index, similar to the customer satisfaction index.

    (5) Strongly Agree   (4) Agree   (3) Somewhat Agree   (2) Disagree   (1) Strongly Disagree

Financial Measures

16. We have identified a few (e.g., 4 to 6) key measures of our overall financial performance.

    (5) Strongly Agree   (4) Agree   (3) Somewhat Agree   (2) Disagree   (1) Strongly Disagree

17. Financial measures are a good mix of short- and long-term measures of financial success.

    (5) Strongly Agree   (4) Agree   (3) Somewhat Agree   (2) Disagree   (1) Strongly Disagree

18. Financial measures are consistent across different units/locations.

    (5) Strongly Agree   (4) Agree   (3) Somewhat Agree   (2) Disagree   (1) Strongly Disagree

19. We collect financial data on our major competitors to use in evaluating our own performance and in setting goals.

    (5) Strongly Agree   (4) Agree   (3) Somewhat Agree   (2) Disagree   (1) Strongly Disagree

20. The organization aggregates financial data into one or two summary statistics that reflect overall performance, such as economic value-added (EVA) or return on assets (ROA).

    (5) Strongly Agree   (4) Agree   (3) Somewhat Agree   (2) Disagree   (1) Strongly Disagree

Operational Measures

21. The organization has developed a set of 4 to 6 common operational measures such as value added per employee that are used in all locations/functions.

    (5) Strongly Agree   (4) Agree   (3) Somewhat Agree   (2) Disagree   (1) Strongly Disagree

22. Any process measures that are collected are directly related to key product/service characteristics that customers care about.

    (5) Strongly Agree   (4) Agree   (3) Somewhat Agree   (2) Disagree   (1) Strongly Disagree

23. Cycle time is used as a key operational measure throughout the organization.

    (5) Strongly Agree   (4) Agree   (3) Somewhat Agree   (2) Disagree   (1) Strongly Disagree

24. Operational measures allow us to prevent problems rather than just identify them.

    (5) Strongly Agree   (4) Agree   (3) Somewhat Agree   (2) Disagree   (1) Strongly Disagree

25. The organization has established measurable standards for all key process measures.

    (5) Strongly Agree   (4) Agree   (3) Somewhat Agree   (2) Disagree   (1) Strongly Disagree

Supplier Measures

26. The organization has a rating system for evaluating supplier performance.

    (5) Strongly Agree   (4) Agree   (3) Somewhat Agree   (2) Disagree   (1) Strongly Disagree

27. Our supplier rating system is a mix of hard data such as products returned/shipments rejected, and soft measures such as our satisfaction levels with suppliers' responsiveness.

    (5) Strongly Agree   (4) Agree   (3) Somewhat Agree   (2) Disagree   (1) Strongly Disagree

28. The quality of goods and services purchased from suppliers is measured on a regular basis.

    (5) Strongly Agree   (4) Agree   (3) Somewhat Agree   (2) Disagree   (1) Strongly Disagree

29. Our organization asks suppliers for process data and encourages self-inspection.

    (5) Strongly Agree   (4) Agree   (3) Somewhat Agree   (2) Disagree   (1) Strongly Disagree

30. Staying within our price guidelines is only one of many measures used to evaluate and select suppliers.

    (5) Strongly Agree   (4) Agree   (3) Somewhat Agree   (2) Disagree   (1) Strongly Disagree

Product/Service Quality Measures

31. Characteristics of products/services that are measured are those that are most important to customers.

    (5) Strongly Agree   (4) Agree   (3) Somewhat Agree   (2) Disagree   (1) Strongly Disagree

32. If 100 percent of products/services are not checked, then large enough sample sizes are used to ensure that all products/services meet standards.

    (5) Strongly Agree   (4) Agree   (3) Somewhat Agree   (2) Disagree   (1) Strongly Disagree

33. Automated measurement devices are used wherever possible to avoid errors caused by poor human judgment.

    (5) Strongly Agree   (4) Agree   (3) Somewhat Agree   (2) Disagree   (1) Strongly Disagree

34. Measures for services are related to accomplishments rather than behaviors (e.g., percent of correct orders filled or percent of flights that take off on time vs. smiling when greeting a customer).

    (5) Strongly Agree   (4) Agree   (3) Somewhat Agree   (2) Disagree   (1) Strongly Disagree

35. Measures of product/service quality are expressed as actual numbers rather than percentages of defect-free products/services.

    (5) Strongly Agree   (4) Agree   (3) Somewhat Agree   (2) Disagree   (1) Strongly Disagree

Safety/Environmental/Public Responsibility Measures

36. The organization collects data on safety and environmental performance at least once a month, using several different metrics.

    (5) Strongly Agree   (4) Agree   (3) Somewhat Agree   (2) Disagree   (1) Strongly Disagree

37. Measures of safety are more behavioral and preventive in nature rather than the typical lost-time accidents.

    (5) Strongly Agree   (4) Agree   (3) Somewhat Agree   (2) Disagree   (1) Strongly Disagree

38. Environmental measures go beyond those mandated by the EPA and other regulatory agencies.

    (5) Strongly Agree   (4) Agree   (3) Somewhat Agree   (2) Disagree   (1) Strongly Disagree

39. The organization collects data on regulatory matters and measures of public responsibility such as hours of community service or awards received from community/civic groups.

    (5) Strongly Agree   (4) Agree   (3) Somewhat Agree   (2) Disagree   (1) Strongly Disagree

40. The organization has developed a public responsibility index that is an aggregation of safety, environmental, and community service measures.

    (5) Strongly Agree   (4) Agree   (3) Somewhat Agree   (2) Disagree   (1) Strongly Disagree

Part III: Reporting and Analyzing Data

41. The organization reports data from all sections of its scorecard in a single report to all key managers.

    (5) Strongly Agree   (4) Agree   (3) Somewhat Agree   (2) Disagree   (1) Strongly Disagree

42. Data are presented graphically in an easy-to-read format that requires minimal analysis to identify trends and levels of performance.

    (5) Strongly Agree   (4) Agree   (3) Somewhat Agree   (2) Disagree   (1) Strongly Disagree

43. Data on customer satisfaction, employee satisfaction, and innovation/growth are reviewed as often and by the same executives as data on financial, operational, product/service, and supplier performance.

    (5) Strongly Agree   (4) Agree   (3) Somewhat Agree   (2) Disagree   (1) Strongly Disagree

44. The organization has done research to identify correlations between customer satisfaction levels and financial performance.

    (5) Strongly Agree   (4) Agree   (3) Somewhat Agree   (2) Disagree   (1) Strongly Disagree

45. The organization understands the relationships between all the key measures in its overall scorecard.

    (5) Strongly Agree   (4) Agree   (3) Somewhat Agree   (2) Disagree   (1) Strongly Disagree

46. Performance data are analyzed and used to make key decisions about the organization's business.

    (5) Strongly Agree   (4) Agree   (3) Somewhat Agree   (2) Disagree   (1) Strongly Disagree

47. The key measures are consistent with the organization's mission, values, and long-term goals and strategies.

(5) Strongly Agree   (4) Agree   (3) Somewhat Agree   (2) Disagree   (1) Strongly Disagree

48. The organization continuously evaluates and improves its measures and the methods used to collect and report performance data.

(5) Strongly Agree   (4) Agree   (3) Somewhat Agree   (2) Disagree   (1) Strongly Disagree

49. Automated and human (e.g., surveys/checklists) measurement devices are calibrated on a regular basis to ensure accuracy and reliability.

(5) Strongly Agree   (4) Agree   (3) Somewhat Agree   (2) Disagree   (1) Strongly Disagree

50. The measures in the organization's scorecard are the same ones on which annual and longer-term goals are set during the planning process.

(5) Strongly Agree   (4) Agree   (3) Somewhat Agree   (2) Disagree   (1) Strongly Disagree

Calculating Your Score

Questions 1 to 5 relate to your entire measurement system, so they are worth more than the rest of the questions. Add up the total for questions 1 to 5, and multiply this number by 2. A perfect score would be 50, if you answered "Strongly Agree" for all five questions. Write the total for questions 1 to 5 in the space below. Proceed by adding up the total for questions 6 to 40. Next, add up the total points for questions 41 to 50, and multiply this number by 2. Add up the three numbers to come out with the final total. A perfect score on this assessment is 325, so if you ended up with more than that, go back and check your math.

Total questions 1 to 5:   _____ × 2 = _____

Total questions 6 to 40:   + _____

Total questions 41 to 50:   + _____ × 2 = _____

Grand total: ___/325___

Interpreting Your Score

Scores of 276 to 325

If your score on this survey is in this top band, you truly have a world-class approach to measuring your organization's performance. You have narrowed down your database to a few key metrics and must have a well-balanced set of metrics. It also is evident that you actually use the data you collect to make decisions about improving organizational performance. Yours should be an organization that others benchmark for measurement. In fact, you might want to consider sending this book to a friend who works in an organization that is not quite as sophisticated as yours when it comes to measurement.

Scores of 226 to 275

If your score is in this second band, you have a systematic approach to measurement that approaches being well-balanced. Chances are you are weak in measures of customer satisfaction and employee satisfaction, and may not do a good job of aggregating individual metrics into summary statistics and analyzing the data to improve organizational performance. You have made a great deal of progress in improving your organization's approach to measurement. However, additional refinement is needed over time, and more research needs to be done to identify correlations between long-term measures such as customer satisfaction/employee satisfaction and shorter-term measures such as financial performance. Being in this band probably means that your measurement system is better than 75 to 80 percent of organizations in North America.

Scores of 176 to 225

A score in this range puts you in about the middle, which says that you are off to a good start in reengineering your approach to measurement. You probably have a good set of measures for some of the seven boxes on an organization's scorecard. You also probably have some major weaknesses in some types of measures. You are probably strong in financial, operational, and product/service quality data, and weak in the other four areas. Chances are you still have too many measures and have inconsistencies across the different units/locations in your organization. A score in this range says that you are making some refinements in your approach to measurement but still need to do quite a bit of work to put together a good solid measurement approach.

Scores of 175 or Less

This puts you at the 50 percent or below score level, which means that you are a long way from having a balanced scorecard. You're in good company at this level, however. In my experience, this is where most businesses are, and where almost all government and healthcare organizations are. Most business organizations are only just starting to measure customer satisfaction and employee satisfaction. Government and healthcare organizations are weak in these two areas, and also tend to be weak in product/service quality data, and measures of supplier performance. Organizations that score less than 50 percent on this survey probably still have not convinced upper management that strategic longer-term measures are just as important as the traditional financial and operational metrics. In any event, I suggest that you keep reading and try to apply some of the concepts in this book to improve your approach to measurement.

Part

Selecting the Right Metrics

Keeping Score in World-Class Organizations

4

This second part of the book is about developing measures for the different categories of metrics on your organizational scorecard. Your measurement system should consist of six different categories of data:

1. Financial performance.
2. Product/service quality.
3. Supplier performance.
4. Customer satisfaction.
5. Process and operational performance.
6. Employee satisfaction.

The specific categories you select to include on your scorecard are not as important as the fact that they represent a balance between the needs and requirements of your shareholders, stakeholders, customers, and employees. It is also important that your metrics are balanced between past and future-oriented measures. In other words, you need to select metrics that help tell you how well you are progressing toward achieving your long-term vision.

SELECTING THE CATEGORIES OF DATA ON YOUR SCORECARD

The categories of data you select to include on your scorecard should be dictated by the type of business you are in and the key success factors for your organization. For example, the Department of Energy's largest nuclear waste disposal site in Richland, Washington, should have a separate category of metrics that relates to employee and public safety. In a bank or financial services firm, a separate category of data for employee safety is probably not needed. A firm that must continuously come up with new products to grow and survive might have a separate category of data that relates to new product developments and launches.

There are certain generic categories of data that should be included on any organization's scorecard. For example, all organizations need to have financial performance data, customer satisfaction data, and probably some collection of employee well-being and satisfaction data. Even organizations that spend relatively little money on labor, such as the steel companies, need to have employee satisfaction metrics on their scorecard. The other categories of data you select for your scorecard should be based on your key business drivers or success factors. These are factors that you need to focus on to differentiate yourself from your competitors. A chemical company, for example, has a box on its scorecard that relates to competitive pricing and value, because that is one of its key advantages over the competition. It has chosen to be the low-cost supplier of commodity chemicals, so it has a number of metrics that tell how it is doing on price relative to its competitors and how customers perceive its pricing. This same company is attempting to grow by adding new products each year and expanding sales to international customers. Hence, it has a category of metrics on its scorecard that relates to growth through new product development and sales to overseas customers.

MEASURING FINANCIAL PERFORMANCE

One type of data that all organizations need to have on their scorecard is financial performance. Even nonprofit and government organizations need to be concerned with budget performance and cost control. The challenge in this section of your scorecard is not in selecting good measurable statistics, but in narrowing them down to only a few. It is also important that the financial metrics that are selected do more than just measure the past. Focusing on quarterly profits or earnings is fine, but this is water under the bridge. A good set of financial metrics needs to measure the past, the present, and the future. Developing good metrics that focus on future financial success is a tricky business. Wall Street analysts have been trying to come up with good predictive ratios or financial metrics that predict the future for years, and they have not hit on any one magic number.

Companies like AT&T and Coca-Cola claim that economic value-added (EVA) is the one financial metric that will help a company measure its performance and build value for its shareholders. However, it's unlikely that focusing on any one measure has made either of these companies so successful by itself. In Chapter 5, I'll discuss financial performance in more detail, along with some of the newer financial metrics like EVA and MVA.

MEASURING CUSTOMER SATISFACTION AND VALUE

This is an area of weakness in many organizations' scorecards. Many have only just now begun to measure customer satisfaction, and most are doing it in a very rudimentary fashion. Many conduct an annual survey that asks a series of generic questions, receive the data, and are not sure what to do about them. Leading organizations like IBM, Ford, and AT&T spend a great deal of time and money designing and continuously improving methods for measuring customer satisfaction. The key to a good customer satisfaction measurement system is to have a good mix of data on customer opinions and their actual buying behavior. The soft or opinion data should help to identify problems early so they can be corrected, and the hard data on buying behavior lets you know whether or not what customers say about your products and services actually relates to their buying behavior. A number of companies have a difficult time linking customer satisfaction levels with market share and repeat business.

Along with customer satisfaction, it is also important to measure customer value. Value is a ratio of satisfaction over perception of the fairness of the price. I can be extremely satisfied with the quality of a $150 dinner, but feel ripped off and never return to the restaurant. Perceived value is just as important as satisfaction and has to be included in your overall customer satisfaction measurement system.

MEASURING PRODUCT AND SERVICE QUALITY

Measuring the quality of your products or services by waiting for feedback from customers is a risky approach. All organizations also need internal metrics that tell them that they have high-quality products and services before they ship them or deliver them to customers. The focus in this section of your scorecard should be the vital few key quality indices that relate back to the most important requirements of your customers.

Often, these dimensions are the most difficult to measure. In an advertising agency, the quality of a television commercial may be judged on its uniqueness and its ability to be memorable, rather than technical dimensions such as production quality or whether it was completed on schedule. Internal quality metrics need to be tracked on a regular basis to ensure that customers only receive high-quality goods and services.

The problem with product/service quality data is narrowing it down to the vital few. A complicated product or service is often measured on more than 100 quality variables that are all important to customers. Even a simple service like preparing a dinner for a room-service customer in a hotel can involve the measurement of many variables. Rather than eliminating the wide variety of product/service quality metrics that you currently collect and control, try to aggregate these individual metrics into overall indices that help provide a big picture of overall quality levels. More on this in Chapter 7.

MEASURING PROCESSES AND OPERATIONAL PERFORMANCE

Rather than focus on simply measuring product or service quality, it is also important to measure in-process metrics that help you predict whether you might have a problem with your output metrics. Process or operational metrics are proactive or preventive in nature and focus on work activity as it is occurring. Many organizations focus only on measuring the outputs rather than the processes used to produce those outputs. In a business where what they do is almost a science, process metrics are easy to come up with and usually are very good predictors of the quality of the outputs produced. For example, a paper mill or steel mill both run with relatively few people; many key process variables are monitored and controlled by equipment and computers rather than by people. In other types of organizations, there is much more art and less science in what they do. Therefore, selecting the correct process variables becomes tricky. Performance on process measures can look very good, whereas output measures show poor performance levels. Recall the story of Lynn and Larry from Chapter 2.

MEASURING SUPPLIER PERFORMANCE

Outsourcing has become a major trend in organizations today. For many, if it is not a core competency, a function is outsourced. Companies are outsourcing their entire management information systems functions, or their customer service functions, and firms are popping up all over that promise to perform these support services better and for less expense than internal functions. Along with this trend toward outsourcing, there are all the regular goods and services that companies have historically purchased from outside suppliers. A chemical company, for example, spends 66¢ of every dollar of expense on outside suppliers. What all of this says is that organizations need to have a very thorough method for measuring supplier performance.

Most manufacturing organizations do incoming inspections of supplier goods, but I'm talking about a much more comprehensive approach than this. A number of companies have very sophisticated approaches to measuring the performance of key suppliers. Boeing, for example, is known for its rigorous approach of monitoring suppliers on a wide variety of process and output performance metrics. Pacific Bell has been benchmarked by many others for its approach to measuring supplier performance. In fact, Pacific Bell's approach has been adopted by American Express as its method for tracking supplier performance. A good set of supplier metrics includes measures of product/service quality, process variables, price competitiveness, and overall ease of doing business.

MEASURING EMPLOYEE WELL-BEING AND SATISFACTION

This is the section of most organizations' scorecard that is by far the weakest. The human resources manager may track statistics like turnover and conduct an annual morale or climate survey, but often these data are not included in the overall performance metrics that executives review on a regular basis. A few forward-thinking organizations believe that the health and satisfaction levels of their employees are just as important as an indicator of overall health as are their financial metrics. Some of these organizations have also found that focusing on employee satisfaction pays off on the bottom line. Home Depot is known for paying its employees up to 25 percent more than its competitors, providing much more training and putting a lot of effort into making the store a good place to work. It is also able to offer customers the most competitive prices on just about everything, the biggest selection of merchandise, and a level of service that is difficult to find anywhere else. Their shareholders have also been quite happy with Home Depot's performance as well.

Few organizations would argue with the idea that employee health and well-being is important to a successful business. However, few have determined a good way of tracking this area of performance on a regular basis. Waiting until an employee quits or until the once-a-year climate survey is done to obtain data on employee morale is hardly an adequate approach. Companies like AT&T and Federal Express have developed very good metrics that tell them about the health and well-being of their workforce.

MEASURING LEARNING, INNOVATION, AND GROWTH

Most of today's organizations need to become more flexible, innovative, take more risks, and generally do things that will help ensure their future success. You will find the words "growth, innovation, and risk-taking" in the values of a great many organizations. Yet, few do a good job of measuring how well they take risks or come up with new ideas. Kaplan and Norton, whose articles on the balanced scorecard approach to measurement are referenced throughout this text, suggest that all organizations need a separate category on their scorecards for innovation and growth metrics. Some example metrics that one might find in this category include:

- Number of suggestions by employees

- Percentage of suggestions implemented

- Return on investment from process improvement or reengineering projects

- Number of patents received

- Number of innovation-related awards received for products or services

- Growth in the competency levels of employees

- Percentage of employees cross-trained to perform three or more jobs

- Overall score on Malcolm Baldrige assessment (used to identify world-class companies).

Having a separate category of measures that are future- or innovation-based may not be necessary, but it certainly does help draw attention to the need for future-oriented metrics on an organization's scorecard. If you prefer not to have a separate category for these types of metrics, they could just as easily fit under other categories I have previously described. I have not included a separate chapter on future-oriented metrics, but discuss them within other segments of the scorecard.

MAKING SURE YOU HAVE SELECTED THE RIGHT METRICS

I've seen a few organizations that claim to now have a balanced scorecard because they have begun measuring nonfinancial areas of performance. If it were only that simple. Selecting the right performance measures takes a great deal of thought and strategizing. All organizations need to have a balanced set of metrics that addresses the needs of customers, shareholders, stakeholders, and employees, but the exact metrics that are selected can make the difference between success and failure. The most important rule to keep in mind when putting together your organization's scorecard is to make sure the metrics link back to the key success factors and business fundamentals that are linked to your organization's success.

Measuring Financial Performance

A new value-based revolution in finance is providing a practical framework that managers can use to build a premium-valued company.

—G. Bennett Stewart III

If you had to pick at least one area of your company's scorekeeping approach where you have good measures, it would be financial, right? Chances are you have no shortage of financial data on the traditional measures: profit, ROI, income, expenses, cash flow, stock prices, accounts receivable, accounts payable, and so on. Every business is required to keep certain financial records for tax purposes, but doesn't that mean that these are the right measures for running a business? Not necessarily. The problem with most companies' approach to measuring financial performance is that they measure too many things, and too few of the measures are data that are useful in managing performance in the organization. In other words, most financial reports do not contain the right amount or the right data that managers need to make good business decisions and effectively run the organization.

EVERYONE KNOWS THE GAME

If there's one thing that American executives are good at, it's manipulating an organization's expenses to improve short-term profitability. A new executive comes in to take over a failing business unit. Her first task is to remove costs from the business. This is normally done by reducing head count, because labor is one of the few variable-cost items that can be manipulated without directly impacting income. So, the new boss lays off 10 to 20 percent of the workforce, cuts overtime, and all of a sudden the bottom line starts improving. She reduces the cost of purchased goods and services by putting the squeeze on suppliers or finding new ones, and reduces other big-ticket cost items like real estate by getting rid of offices. As a result of all this cost-cutting, profits really do improve, but often at the expense of quality, morale, and customer satisfaction.

Because organizations have been measuring financial performance in practically the same way for the last 30 years, executives also have learned to play games with the numbers to make their organizations look good. When $100,000 bonuses are at stake, there is a real incentive to make the numbers look good. Creative accounting techniques are often applied to ensure that executives still receive their big bonuses. All this playing around with cost reduction and creative accounting usually results in a promotion for the executive. She moves on to a bigger and better job with a bigger salary, and someone new inherits the mess that was created when employee morale problems explode or customers start buying from the competition because of poor quality. However, the game continues with a new crop of executives who come in every few years and play around with the numbers again to make them look good. Not all of this is a charade. Many organizations do need to cut their head counts and expenses. Some of these reductions can result in the company being more efficient on a longer-term basis. However, cost-cutting by itself will not secure an organization's future success. In this chapter, we will explore some new techniques for measuring financial performance and describe the characteristics of an effective financial measurement database.

THREE PERSPECTIVES: YESTERDAY, TODAY, AND TOMORROW

A sound approach to financial measurement is to make sure that your data base includes three types of information:

1. *Historical Data:* How did we do last month, last week, this year, last year, and so on?

2. *Current Data:* How are we doing right now, today?

3. *Future Data:* How will we be doing in the next few months or years?

From a financial standpoint, the purpose of a business is to create wealth for its owners. Output measures or historical financial measures help an organization keep score of how well it is doing at creating wealth. These data are always past-focused because they are based on events that have already occurred: our net profit for the year versus last year, our sales revenue this year versus last year, and our average stock price this month versus last month. These are all measures of corporate performance that are based on history. Any financial information that goes into a report to shareholders or other stakeholders would typically fall into the category of historical data.

Historical data are interesting, but do not enable a manager to do much to improve future performance. Historical data are water under the bridge. A manager needs to pay attention to all three perspectives: yesterday, today, and tomorrow. Peter Drucker calls these measures of today's financial performance *foundation measures* ("The Information Executives Truly Need," *Harvard Business Review,* January/February 1995), and explains that this type of data

> may be likened to the measurements a doctor takes at a routine physical: weight, pulse, blood pressure, temperature, and urine analysis. If those readings are normal, they do not tell us much. If they are abnormal, they indicate a problem that needs to be identified and treated. Those measurements might be called foundation information. (p. 58)

Some typical vital signs for a business might be cash flow, orders in the pipeline, total dollars in accounts receivable, and daily sales figures.

Another measure of today's financial results is the amount of cash the business has on hand or the total value of its assets as compared with its liabilities. This is a good measure of an organization's overall financial health. For a nonprofit organization, a financial metric from the current perspective might be the amount of budget money that is remaining. These types of financial metrics should answer the question: How are we doing today?

The third type of financial data needed in a complete set of measures is used to predict the company's future financial performance. Air Products and Chemicals uses percentage of total sales that come from new products as a financial measure that is future-focused. Consulting and accounting firms typically use the dollar value of outstanding proposals as a financial statistic to predict their future health. They also typically put a percentage on each proposal based on the likelihood that each will be awarded to them. These forecasts are used to plan for future workload and resource requirements. Another common future-oriented financial statistic is dollars invested in research and development as a ratio to sales revenue or profit. Organizations often cut back on these costs during tough times, which may cause them to mortgage their future for the sake of short-term financial gains. Growth in sales from a particular geographic region or a particular industry may also be a future-oriented financial statistic if the company is looking to grow into new or emerging markets.

Arthur Andersen's Steve Hronec calls this future-oriented financial data *strategic measures* and defines it as

> [T]he cost information needed to make decisions that will have long-term effects on the company. Examples of strategic cost information include make/buy decisions, target cost analysis, and product cost analysis. (*Vital Signs,* New York: AMACOM Press, 1993, p. 131)

ECONOMIC VALUE-ADDED (EVA): THE KEY TO CREATING WEALTH AND IMPROVING FINANCIAL PERFORMANCE

Ask the CEOs of AT&T, Coca-Cola, CSX, and Quaker Oats what they would measure if they could only look at one measure of a company's financial health. They would tell you EVA, or economic value-added. EVA is a more accurate way of measuring a company's profitability. It is more accurate than traditional profit measures, because it includes the cost of capital in the equation. Capital is money that is tied up in equipment and buildings, as well as investments in training, research and development, and other things designed to pay off over more than a single year. Capital also includes working capital such as cash, inventories, and receivables. Hence, a company can be operating at a profit according to the balance sheet, but actually be operating at a loss if one includes the cost of the capital needed to run the business. Therefore, profit can be a very misleading factor in measuring financial success. We have all heard about companies that were profitable for years and are now out of business.

The formula for computing EVA is shown in Table 5.1. The first two entries in the table show companies with positive EVA statistics, whereas the last one shows a negative EVA. All three companies show healthy profits as a percentage of total sales, but calculating their EVA performance is much more revealing than simply looking at profits.

TABLE 5.1   Calculating EVA

Operating Profit ($ million)		Taxes ($ million)		Cost of Capital ($ million)	EVA ($ million)
250	minus	87	minus	110	53 +
1,750	minus	670	minus	840	240 +
18	minus	4.2	minus	16.5	2.7 −

If you had to pick one historical index to measure, EVA should probably be it. Using this measure helps you avoid bad investments and leads you to better decisions about how to run your business. According to a report in *Fortune* magazine (September 20, 1993), concentrating on EVA has dramatically improved stock prices at AT&T, Coca-Cola, and others, thus increasing the value of these companies. Watching EVA has also helped the companies make better business decisions about spending money. Quaker Oats CEO William Smithburg explains that

> EVA makes managers act like shareholders. It's the true corporate faith of the 1990s. (p. 38)

The most complete reference on EVA is a book entitled *The Quest for Value* by G. Bennett Stewart III (New York: Harper Business School Press, 1991). In fact, Stewart, a financial consultant, is credited with popularizing EVA as a better measure of company financial performance. Like most things in the management world, EVA is not new. In fact, Peter Drucker says he discussed EVA at length in his 1964 book *Managing for Results.* He also cites two other authors who discussed it in a book published in the 1890s. Although, EVA is hardly new, it is new to most business people. Not many had read Stewart's book until *Fortune* magazine ran a cover story on EVA in its issue of September 20, 1993, dubbing EVA "Today's hottest financial idea and getting hotter." Now, Stewart and his New York consulting firm are in demand by some of the most forward-thinking CEOs in the world. Stewart explains that using EVA as a key performance metric, and linking management compensation to EVA, creates an incentive for managers to:

> 1. Improve operating profits without tying up any more operating capital.

2. Draw down more capital on the line of credit so long as
    the additional profits management earns by investing
    the capital cover the charge for the additional capital.

3. Free up capital and pay down the line of credit so long
    as any earnings lost are more than offset by savings on
    the capital charge. (*The Quest for Value,* p. 225)

You probably do not have a choice but to continue measuring traditional
financial accounting metrics and completing a monthly balance sheet that
summarizes the company's performance. However, EVA is the one statistic that really matters. It is subordinate to all others on the balance sheet.

MARKET VALUE-ADDED (MVA): ANOTHER NEW WAY OF LOOKING AT FINANCIAL PERFORMANCE

EVA has received a lot of press coverage in the last few years as another
magic bullet that will help transform ailing companies into profitable
ones. EVA's lesser known brother is another statistic called market value-
added (MVA). Another measure that has been devised by consultants at
Stern Stewart in New York, MVA is thought to be the best indicator of a
company's ability to create wealth for its shareholders. According to
"The New Champ of Wealth Creation" (*Fortune,* September 18, 1995), it
is not just another three-letter acronym for a new management fad or a
measurement index that requires a Ph.D. to understand. Like EVA, MVA
is a ratio. On the top half of the ratio is all the capital the company has invested since it began. The bottom figure of the ratio is the market value of
all the company's equity and debt. If the market value is less than the top
figure of the money invested, the company's managers have obviously
destroyed the investors' capital.

The *Fortune* article lists Coca-Cola as the top-scoring company on
the MVA scale for 1995. Others in the top five include General Electric,
Wal-Mart, Merck, and Microsoft. It is interesting that GE and Coca-Cola,
the two top MVA companies, have created most of their success in less
than 15 years. CEO Goizueta at Coke has taken his company from $1.8
billion in MVA in 1981 to $59 billion in 1995. Jack Welch at GE has
taken his company from a negative MVA of $387 million in 1981 to a
positive MVA of $52 billion. Consultants from Stern Stewart suggest that
both EVA and MVA be used as the basis for executive bonuses. The real

job of an executive is to create wealth for the company owners, and both of these statistics measure how well this is being accomplished. Of course, executive compensation needs to be linked to a balance of other nonfinancial metrics as well, but MVA and EVA ought to be heavy hitters in the bonus calculation formula.

ACTIVITY-BASED COSTING (ABC): A NEW WAY OF LOOKING AT DAILY FINANCIAL PERFORMANCE

Just as EVA is a new way of looking at historical or past financial performance, activity-based costing (ABC) is a new method for calculating the real costs of doing business on a daily basis. ABC is similar to EVA because both are more accurate ways of measuring true financial performance. ABC is a method for tracking all costs associated with producing good and services, not just those costs that traditional accounting methods dictate. In addition to the cost of actually producing a product, the ABC approach involves measuring the cost of machine downtime, the cost of inventory waiting to be shipped, and the cost of reworking or scrapping bad product. ABC came along about the same time and partially as a result of the process analysis and improvement movement. As organizations began drawing flow charts or models of their processes, they also began calculating the true cost of each major step in their processes. This allowed them to make improvements in their processes where they could reduce costs the most and not sacrifice the integrity of the process. These analyses also provided important information to the bean counters of the organizations who had never before had a breakdown of the true costs of each step in major production and distribution processes.

The real value of the ABC approach is in how it allocates costs to specific activities or process steps, rather than to the traditional accounting categories. Traditional cost accounting categories are too broad to be of much use in reducing costs or in diagnosing problems. For example, looking at the cost of indirect labor is not very revealing unless one knows what work that indirect labor was used to complete. Essentially, ABC is a way of breaking down cost items into a greater degree of detail so managers can evaluate the appropriateness of the spending that goes on in their organizations. By combining ABC data with process analysis, reengineering or process improvement techniques can be used to focus on eliminating steps that cost a great deal; they may add little or no value to the product or service.

The key to achieving good-quality products or services is to control the processes involved in producing those products or services. Similarly, the key to achieving good-quality financial results such as EVA or profits is to bring in enough income and control your costs of running the business. ABC data provide you with the process data needed to get a true picture of your costs so you can manage them more effectively. Thus, achieving excellent financial results is largely a matter of having true cost data and knowing how to control the performance variables that consume costs.

Because ABC provides a truer picture of your real costs of doing business on a daily basis, I thoroughly recommend this approach as a way of measuring your financial performance. Will it solve all your problems? Hardly. It will cost money to implement, and a few organizations have found that the effort involved in switching to ABC did not pay off in better cost control. Don't let that discourage you, though. Most who have adopted this approach have reaped many benefits.

COST OF QUALITY

Phil Crosby's success is largely based on his concept of tracking the true costs of quality goods and services. Crosby suggested to executives that their existing accounting systems did not provide them with data on the amount of rework that went into the production and delivery of each of their products and services. The cost of quality (COQ) is a statistic used today by many organizations to track the amount of labor and materials that is expended on rework or the correction of problems. Often, organizations are amazed when they see the true cost of rework. In fact, a German luxury auto maker found that enough rework went into each of its cars in labor and material to build an entire Toyota Camry from scratch. By making management aware of this figure, it became a priority, and the company has made dramatic improvements in its COQ figures in recent years.

What's needed to make COQ work as a reliable statistic is a new time and materials tracking system so that all appropriate costs are allocated to rework. Companies assign different codes to rework labor and materials and teach employees the correct way of tracking rework costs. The problem I've seen is in honest reporting. Once companies decide to focus on reducing the COQ, employees tend to be dishonest in reporting rework, afraid of getting blamed for high COQ costs. Convincing employees that accurate COQ costs are important and that no one will be admonished for high costs in this area take time.

HOW EXCELLENT COMPANIES MEASURE FINANCIAL PERFORMANCE

- A few key financial statistics are used to measure overall organizational performance.

- Financial metrics cover the past, present, and future performance.

- Financial statistics are tightly linked to key success factors.

- Overall financial measures like EVA, MVA, or ROI are used to push profitable growth.

- The organization knows the true costs of its processes and products/services.

- The organization continually evaluates and improves its financial metrics to search for just the right measures that will predict long- and short-term success.

Measuring Customer Satisfaction and Value

IDENTIFYING AND CLASSIFYING CUSTOMERS

Not everybody wants the same things. Customers may all want the basics: good quality at a fair price. Beyond that, there are many differences in what individual customers want and expect from the products and services they buy. An important first step in becoming a customer-focused organization is to do a good job of segmenting customers and determining the needs and desires of each group of customers. For example, Northrop Grumman segments its customers according to whether they are government or commercial, and then further segments customers within these two groups to identify their unique needs and desires.

What's important about the method you use to segment customers is that you group them based on common needs and characteristics, rather than on a scheme that is most convenient for you. For example, a telephone company segments customers into two basic groups: business and residential. Residential customers are all considered the same and not segmented any further. Business customers are divided into three groups: small, medium, and large, based on the revenue they generate for the phone company. This is an unimaginative approach and unlikely to get at the real needs of any group of customers. Not all small businesses have the same requirements for their telephone systems. For example, a distribution company that takes thousands of orders per day by telephone has a very different set of needs for its phone service than does a manufacturing plant with the same number of employees. The telephone company might do a better job if it segmented customers based on their dependence on the telephone to do business or some other factor rather than just small, medium, and large.

DETERMINING CUSTOMER "HOT BUTTONS"

Once you have logically divided your customers into groups or market segments based upon their common needs or characteristics, you need to determine what factors about your products and services are most important to each group. Customers are not just other organizations; they are people. People all have their own idiosyncrasies and biases that you need to be aware of if you are going to sell to them. For example, in my consulting business, I recently had a customer with an unusual requirement. One of the things that mattered most to Charley is that the people that worked for him had well-shined shoes. Shined shoes were one of Charley's "hot buttons." He saw an individual with scuffed unpolished shoes as someone who is unorganized and not on the ball. Being an ex-military man, Charley believed that shined shoes indicated a person was professional and paid attention to details—the key to success in any endeavor. I didn't find out about Charley's hot button by interviewing him on the most important requirements for consultants that he hires—it never came up. I found out about Charley's requirement from one of his people who coached me after our second meeting that Charley made a remark about my shoes after our first meeting, and he noticed Charley eyeing my shoes again in the second meeting. As I was leaving, Charley's assistant advised me to make sure my shoes were shined before our next meeting. At this point, I could get cocky and rebellious and decide that no client is going to judge me on my shoes, or I could be smart and get up 15 minutes early before my next meeting with Charley to shine my shoes . . . which is exactly what I did.

METHODS FOR IDENTIFYING CUSTOMER REQUIREMENTS

The three most common approaches to identifying customer requirements are (1) assume you already know what customers want, (2) ask customers what they want and expect, and (3) determine their requirements through their feedback and by seeing what they complain about. None of these approaches is very effective.

How Making Assumptions Can Be Dangerous

You've been in this business for 22 years and think that if you didn't know customer needs very well, your company would not have been around as long as it has. Why bother with the expense of focus groups and all these other market research forums to find out what you already know? Some organizations develop new products, services, and features without talking to a single customer. Confident in its knowledge of customer wants and needs, the company designs and introduces new features or services to further delight its customers. Several years ago, I had first-hand experience with a company that assumed it knew how to delight its customers and came up with a new feature for its service. This particular hotel was in the middle of a Total Quality Management initiative and was identifying little extra services it could provide for customers that would make them want to return to this hotel over others in the area. It didn't want to just copy what other hotels did, but to come up with something really unique. What it came up with was unique, all right. Here's how I experienced this new service:

> The wake-up call came at 6:00 A.M. and I jumped out of bed. After flying from the West Coast the night before, I only had about five hours of sleep. I was in the shower for about five minutes when the phone started to ring. I considered answering it, but couldn't imagine who would call me at that hour, and decided they would call back if it was important. The phone continued to ring. After about the tenth ring, I thought maybe I'd better answer it. Maybe it was my client with some news about our meeting or something wrong at home. I jumped out of the shower, almost slipped on the tile floor, and ran dripping to the phone. "Good morning Mr. Brown, we're just calling to make sure that you're up."

Everyone at breakfast in the restaurant was talking about this new service the hotel called the "human snooze alarm," or follow-up wake-up call. Most, however, described it as more annoying than useful. This wonderful new service dreamed up for delighting customers turned out to make most of us very angry. This is the danger of assuming what customers want.

Asking Customers What They Want

Some of the more progressive organizations today do not assume that they know what customers want—they ask them. Focus groups, telephone interviews, mail surveys, and all kinds of methods are used to find out what customers want and expect. Sometimes this works very well. Sometimes a great deal of time and money is invested without much value. Customers tell you they want something, you design a new product around this information, and no one buys it. What happened? People are not very good predictors of their own behavior. They may even think that the product or service you are proposing seems good and that they would buy it. For one reason or another, they just don't buy it, or if they do, end up not liking it as much as they thought. Another problem with using focus groups and similar methods to identify customer requirements is that most customers do not spend much time thinking about car doors or hair conditioners. Customers may respond to your questions with: "I really don't know what I want from a law firm; I guess that you do a good job and charge reasonable rates."

If you employ a market research firm to conduct customer requirements research, you will probably obtain some useful information. It's when companies try to do these things themselves without the expertise that they end up wasting time. If the research is done well, you should end up with a list of all the major things that customers want and expect, along with an indication of the relative importance of each. You probably won't be able to meet all of the customers needs, so it is important to know which ones are the most important.

Using Customer Feedback to Determine Requirements

Many organizations do not employ a proactive approach for identifying requirements. They use customer feedback to determine their customers' hot buttons. If customers start complaining about the format and clarity of your invoices, that feedback is used to initiate improvement efforts. Others don't simply rely on complaints; they survey customers to find out what they liked and didn't like about their products and/or services. Surveys of customer satisfaction do provide data on customer requirements and how well you meet them. However, this is a reactive approach and one that is not very cost-effective. Imagine the company that spends years designing a new feature into its product, introducing it, and advertising it as a great improvement in its product's performance. After using the product, customers almost unanimously hate the new feature, preferring the product the way it was before the company introduced the improvement.

A BETTER BUT RISKIER WAY OF DETERMINING CUSTOMER REQUIREMENTS: STOP EVERYTHING AND SEE WHAT CUSTOMERS ASK FOR

Pete was surprised when he took over the finance and planning function of an organization recently. In looking at what the eight people who worked in Finance and Planning did, Pete determined that they spent about 80 percent of their time inputting data, summarizing it, and preparing reports of mostly financial information for the rest of the organization. He challenged the need for all of these reports; his team informed him that it had conducted several focus groups and individual interviews to identify the information needs of internal customers. The research revealed that people wanted and needed all of the data they were previously sending out, and a few new reports that it had never done before. The Finance and Planning staff explained that they suspected that they were doing the right things all along, but that this customer requirements research proved it.

Pete was skeptical: "You mean that they said they need all of these reports every single month?" "That's right. We're giving them exactly what they ask for, and always meet deadlines on getting them the information in a timely fashion." After thinking about the situation for a few days, Pete decided to take a riskier approach to identifying Finance and Planning's customers' requirements. Pete instructed his staff that it was to stop issuing all reports for two months. His team told him he was nuts. "People need these data to run the organization and make business decisions, Pete. The place will fall apart without these data." Pete said he didn't believe it would and he would take the heat for the decision if it turned out to be a bad one. "We'll document it in our meeting minutes that you guys are going along with this experiment under protest."

So, for two months Pete's team documented some of its key processes, worked on planning, and kept itself busy doing other things besides cranking out financial reports. What do you think happened during the two months when no financial reports were issued? Paul in Service Operations called a couple of times to get some numbers on his labor costs for the month. A couple of Brand Managers called for some sales figures, and some others called for a few key numbers they needed for their functions. This became Pete's customer requirements needs analysis. The data that people called and asked for turned out to be what they really needed to run their functions. Using the information from this nontraditional approach to needs analysis, Pete was able to reduce the amount of data distributed by his department by about 80 percent and reduce the time his people spent inputting and reporting these data by over 50 percent! So, did Pete lay off half of his staff? Nope. He put them to work helping the organization to plan, manage, and control financial performance factors. His people are happier because their work is more challenging and meaningful. Internal customers are happier because they receive only the data they really need to manage their functions, and the overall organization's financial performance is better due to all the additional consulting Pete's staff gives people on how to manage and control their financials.

The point of this true story is that asking customers what they want and need is not the best way of finding out what they really want and need. Pete's staff did this before he took over; customers told the staff they wanted and needed exactly what they were already getting. Reality was that they needed far less data to actually run their functions, however.

COLLECTING GOOD SOFT CUSTOMER SATISFACTION DATA

Although many organizations have no hard measures of customer satisfaction, most have at least some soft data. As mentioned earlier, much of the soft customer satisfaction data are misleading or incomplete. A balanced set of scores relating to customer satisfaction should include three or four individual metrics based upon different measurement methods. All organizations should do some type of customer satisfaction survey to ask customers to rate their overall customer satisfaction with the entire organization, as well as with specific products/services and people/functions. Any customer satisfaction survey ought to contain questions similar to those listed in Figure 6.1.

You will notice that three of the five questions in Figure 6.1 ask customers to rate their satisfaction on some scale, and that two of the questions are open-ended, requiring a brief answer. Both types of questions are good. The rating questions allow you to quantify overall ratings from customers and to track trends over time. The open-ended questions solicit specific information that can be used for improvement, but is difficult to quantify.

FIGURE 6.1 Standard Customer Satisfaction Survey Questions

1. Overall, how would you rate the quality of our products/services?

2. How would you rate our responsiveness to your problems/concerns?

3. How easy are we to do business with?

4. What products/services should we offer that are not currently offered?

5. What is one thing we could do to improve your level of satisfaction?

THE WRONG WAY OF USING SCALES TO DETERMINE CUSTOMER SATISFACTION LEVELS

The most common approach for having customers rate their overall satisfaction is to use the scale shown in Figure 6.2. Ratings are tabulated and averaged to yield a total score such as 3.85/5.0. IBM uses a little different approach with a 100-point scale. A score of 100 on its Net Satisfaction Index would indicate that 100 percent of the customers surveyed gave IBM a "very satisfied," the highest rating on its scale.

A real estate company summarizes its customer satisfaction data as percent of customers satisfied. Trade magazine ads claim that the company has a 96 percent customer satisfaction level. Knowing that it uses a 5-point scale like the one in Figure 6.2, I asked how it calculates percent satisfied. The answer: anything 2 or above. My next question was: What percentage of 2s, 3s, 4s, and 5s do you get? "Our software doesn't allow

FIGURE 6.2 Customer Satisfaction Scale

5	4	3	2	1
Outstanding	Very Good	Satisfactory	Fair	Poor

us to break out the data that way." Further explanation revealed that it was not really interested in the breakout. It turns out that it is standard practice in the real estate business to measure percent satisfied customers by counting 2–5 ratings. All other real estate companies do it that way, too. It also turned out that the company pays bonuses to most employees for customer satisfaction levels. Guess what the goal is for receiving a bonus? 95 percent or above. So, this company pays out bonuses for what may be poor performance. The measurement and reporting system drives mediocrity because it gives people credit for receiving a 2 or 3 rating. There is no incentive to get customers to rate the organization a 4 or 5 because it does not track this.

Another way to stack the deck to ensure that you look good on customer satisfaction surveys is in how you ask the questions. Even the Department of Motor Vehicles (DMV) is into improving customer satisfaction these days. One of the biggest complaints people have about the DMV is that they have to wait too long in too many lines to renew their drivers licenses or plates. So one state's DMV began working to reduce waiting time; it surveyed customers to determine how they felt about the wait time. The survey asks the question like this:

Based on your past experience at the DMV, was your wait in line today reasonable or not?

( ) YES   ( ) NO

The DMV was very proud that about 65 percent of its "customers" responded to the survey question with a "yes" answer. There are two big problems with this question. First of all, by starting the question with "Based on your past experience at the DMV," they are already establishing a bias toward a positive response. I don't know about you, but I would guess that most people waited in line a long time the last time they visited the DMV. If this time you only waited 45 minutes and the last time it was an hour and a half, you would answer the question with a "yes" response. The second problem with this question is the use of a yes/no scale and the word "reasonable." What does reasonable mean? Some people I've talked to have said that if they can renew their drivers license in less than an hour, that is reasonable. If the DMV really wanted to find out where it stood, rather than just elicit a positive response, here's how it should have asked the question:

Please check the total amount of time you spent at the DMV today, renewing your driver's license or your auto tags.

( ) 90 minutes or more   ( ) 60–90 minutes
( ) 30–60 minutes   ( ) 30 minutes or less

THE RIGHT WAY TO USE SCALES TO MEASURE CUSTOMER SATISFACTION

The real estate and DMV examples are set up to produce misleadingly high ratings and drive or actually reward mediocre levels of customer satisfaction. The system to be described does just the opposite—it drives delighting customers, not merely satisfying them. The difference between the two types of customers is that satisfied customers are on the fence, and may leave for a variety of reasons, including just a desire to try something new. Delighted customers, on the other hand, are committed, and are often your best salespeople.

DESIGNING A BALANCED APPROACH TO MEASURING CUSTOMER SATISFACTION

Hard and Soft Measures of Customer Satisfaction

The most important characteristic of a good set of metrics that relates to customer satisfaction is to have a mix of hard and soft measures. Soft measures are measures of customer opinions, perceptions, and feelings. These are your leading-edge indicators that should be used to try and predict customer behavior. Customer opinions and feelings are important. However, these data need to be supplemented with hard measures of customer satisfaction—measures of what customers do, not what they say. For example, gains and losses of customers, market share relative to competitors, and repeat business are all good hard measures of customer satisfaction.

What if your customer base is stable or if you are an internal support function with a captive audience of customers? Hard measures of customer satisfaction are tougher to come up with, but they are still important. An internal training department might measure its "market share" by tracking the training dollars that are spent on outside courses versus those that are spent on internal courses and workshops. A company with a stable base of customers might measure increases and decreases in revenue from existing customers. At least 50 percent of your scorecard for customer satisfaction should be made up of hard measures if you are an organization that provides services to customers who have a choice. In other words, they could take their business elsewhere if they wanted to. Hard measures are more important than soft measures because they reflect customer buying behavior that adds or subtracts money from your organization's coffers. Having all customers rate you as a world-class company won't get you a dime unless they buy something from you.

By themselves, hard measures of customer satisfaction are not enough. By the time a customer is fed up and goes to a competitor, it's too late. I recently closed my business and personal checking accounts at a bank after the eleventh time it deposited my money in the wrong account. Switching banks is a pain for the customer, so I was patient and kept hoping it would get better. I did complain about the deposits several times, but never once received a survey or phone call to ask me how satisfied I was with the bank's service. Measuring lost customers is a good hard measure of customer satisfaction or dissatisfaction for a bank. However, it's not a very good way of preventing problems. That's where the soft data comes in. Customer opinions gathered through surveys, focus groups, and telephone calls help prevent customers from leaving. The soft data tell you that you may have a problem in time to do something about it.

How to Identify Good Hard Measures of Customer Satisfaction

Repeat and lost business are the overall best hard measures of customer satisfaction. However, these data are sometimes very hard to collect. For example, I worked with a major fast-food chain several years ago. At the time, it was struggling to determine the number of customers who go into its stores and never come back because of bad service. This is important data, but difficult to capture. Using its existing measurement system, it could determine revenue per store, and average amount of each check, but it didn't know how many customers were repeat visitors. A more expensive restaurant could track repeat business through credit card receipts or reservations. Fast-food restaurants don't take credit cards though, so how do they find out if customers come back? When I stopped working with this company, it hadn't figured that out. What it was considering was interviewing a random sample of customers as they left the store and asking them about their intentions of returning to the restaurant again, based on their experience. These are soft data. A customer might say she intended to come back but then never return. On the other hand, I've known several people who voiced their intentions never to go back to a restaurant because of the terrible service, but end up going back anyway because they love the food.

Domino's Pizza, another fast-food business, has an excellent system for tracking repeat and lost customers. Once a customer calls a Domino's store, the phone number is listed in a database. Domino's has a computer system tied in with its telephone system that allows it to track and get a printout of customers who have called in more than once. It can also track customers who ordered pizza on a regular basis and then stopped. Its best customers are those who order from Domino's at least six times a month—kind of like the gold frequent fliers of pizza.

Market share is an OK indicator or measure of customer satisfaction. It stands to reason that the more satisfied customers are with your organization, the bigger share of the market you will have. However, market share is influenced by many factors unrelated to customer satisfaction. For example, you could dramatically improve market share because a competitor went out of business, or decide to improve market share by lowering prices to buy your way into a new market. If you do use market share as an indicator of customer satisfaction, I would not give it a high importance rating.

Complaints are not a hard measure of customer satisfaction because a complaint is a record of someone's opinion or feelings. A hard measure of customer satisfaction that a grocery store I'm familiar with uses is the average amount the customer spends in the store each month. The store tracks customer visits through the use of a check cashing card and monitors the amount the customer spends on groceries each visit. If spending increases, the store believes this is an indicator that the customer is spending less money on groceries or related items at other stores. Increased spending could mean that the kids have come home from college, or that the shoppers have finally given up dieting, and have nothing to do with customer satisfaction levels. Similarly, a telephone company measures call volume and revenue as a hard indicator of customer satisfaction. This one is not a good measure. Is the number of calls you make a month and the length of time you talk on the phone in any way related to your satisfaction with the phone company? I don't think so. Of course, if your phone didn't work, you'd stop making calls, but call volume and revenue are not very good indicators for the phone company. Better hard customer satisfaction data might be the number of customers who leave for another long-distance company or the ordering/cancelling of additional services such as call waiting or three-way calling.

A SATISFIED CUSTOMER BUYS FROM YOU: A DELIGHTED CUSTOMER SELLS FOR YOU

A delighted customer is so happy with your products and services that she tells everyone about what a great organization yours is. A satisfied customer is on the fence and may leave at any time for a little better price, or just because he is bored and wants to try something new. A delighted customer is a customer for life—at least as long as you continue to exceed his requirements.

The company whose customer satisfaction measurement system is the toughest I've seen is 1991 Baldrige Award winner Solectron of San José, California. Solectron, a small circuit-board assembler, has customers give them a report card once a month, using letter grades like those used in schools. The company tracks its grade-point average (GPA) every month. In the standard calculation, an A is worth 4.0, a B is worth 3.0, a C, 2.0, and so forth. The Solectron scale is based on the philosophy that a satisfied customer has no value to the company. A satisfied customer is someone who may leave and buy a competitor's products at any time. Therefore, Solectron calculates its GPA as follows:

$$A = \quad 150 \text{ points}$$
$$B = \quad\;\; 50 \text{ points}$$
$$C = \quad\;\;\; 0$$
$$D = -150 \text{ points}$$
$$F = -300 \text{ points}$$

Solectron's scale is set up to promote delighting customers and gives no credit for merely satisfying them.

PUTTING IT ALL TOGETHER: THE CUSTOMER SATISFACTION INDEX

Once you have identified several good hard and soft measures of customer satisfaction, it is a good idea to aggregate all of these data into a single metric: a customer satisfaction index (CSI). A CSI is one of the summary statistics that management can look at every month, or even every week, to determine how well it is satisfying customers. Federal Express reviews its CSI every day and broadcasts scores to all employees via its internal television network. Some general rules about putting together a CSI is that it should:

- Be based on about 50 to 60 percent hard measures and 40 to 50 percent soft measures of customer satisfaction

- Allow you to compute the index at least once a month

- Be able to be broken down by service/product line and location, if necessary

- Be easy to understand by all levels of employees

Each of the individual indices in your CSI should be assigned an importance weight in percentage, based on how important each one is in determining customer satisfaction and buying behavior. For example, complaints might not be given a high weight in the CSI because most customers don't bother complaining, so reduction in complaints may be a misleading indicator. A reduction in complaints could indicate that customer satisfaction has gone down and customers are so fed up, they no longer bother complaining. A sample CSI is shown in Table 6.1.

This system is comprised of 60 percent hard measures of customer buying behavior and 40 percent customer opinions or feelings. Returns are actually a hard measure, but this company chooses to combine it with

TABLE 6.1   Example of Customer Satisfaction Index

Repeat and lost customers	30%
Revenue from existing customers	15%
Market share	15%
Customer satisfaction survey	20%
Complaints/returns	10%
Product-specific surveys	10%
Total	100%

complaint data. Every quarter, the CSI for the entire company is computed, along with CSI levels of individual business units. The CSI is measured on a scale from 0 to 100 points, and levels of performance are set for satisfactory, excellent, and "world-class" levels of performance. Specific improvement goals are set each year and each quarter for the entire company and for each business unit.

MEASURING INTERNAL CUSTOMER SATISFACTION

Internal support functions such as procurement and finance need a balanced set of metrics just like a business unit or an entire organization. However, the approach to segmenting customers and measuring their satisfaction is quite different and nowhere near as involved as for the whole organization. Internal support functions typically have three major types of customers:

1. *Users:* Employees in other functions who use the products and/or services produced by the support functions.

2. *Stakeholders:* Shareholders, bosses, corporate executives, and others who care about the overall health of the organization.

3. *Others Like Us:* Business unit or location support function personnei who provide similar products and services.

The first step is to find out what is most important to each group of customers for each of the major products and services provided for them. Users typically care about things like accuracy, use ability, cost, and timeliness. They may not even care about cost if they don't pay for your services. Stakeholders like the CEO or your boss typically care about overall cost for your function, head count, and managing risk for the entire organization. People in the divisions or locations out of the corporate location who perform similar support functions care about your responsiveness to their needs, providing them with tools that can be used to make their jobs easier and going to bat for them when they need resources.

The most important rule to follow when measuring internal customer satisfaction is to keep it simple and make sure you don't take up much of your internal customer's time. Nine out of ten internal support functions that start measuring customer satisfaction end up dropping the effort within a year or two because they cannot get people to fill out the surveys. As organizations begin trying to change their cultures to be more customer-driven, a few support departments develop their own internal customer satisfaction surveys and begin sending them out. After a couple of years, the effort gains momentum and soon every support function is sending out its own monthly survey asking: "How are we doing?" It gets to the point where many managers are receiving a couple of these surveys every week. They always end up at the bottom of the in-box. Return rates, however, are around 5 to 10 percent until they drop off to nothing. One thing every support function manager has to realize is that most internal customers expect you and your people to do a good job; they don't want to take the time to tell you how you are doing. The only successful internal measures of customer satisfaction are extremely simple and take very little of the customer's time. For example, in one company, internal customers evaluate all support functions using the same five questions very similar to those listed on page 65 once a year. In another company, customer satisfaction is determined by asking one question during regularly scheduled review meetings that occur once a quarter. In both cases, the system works because it demands very little of the customer's time.

Hard measures of customer satisfaction for internal support functions are difficult to come up with unless the support functions act like a profit center. Most support functions have a captive audience of customers. If you need a purchase order, you go through procurement, for example. If your customers have no choice but to go to your support functions, measures of market share or repeat business are inappropriate. If you can come up with hard internal customer satisfaction measures, by all means do so, but don't rack your brain trying to come up with metrics if customers have no choice but to use your services. A customer satisfaction index for a support function such as finance or legal is shown in Table 6.2. Notice that there are no hard measures of internal customer satisfaction in this example and that

TABLE 6.2 Example of an Internal Customer Satisfaction Index for the Corporate Finance Function

Users' customer satisfaction level	45%
Management/stakeholders' satisfaction	30%
Field/location finance satisfaction	25%
Total	100%

weights are given to each of the three groups of customers. This is important because sometimes two customers have conflicting needs. Upper management may want you to select a particular company as a supplier to meet your quota for small business suppliers, whereas the people who will use the supplier's services may want to continue using the large company they have been using that is doing an outstanding job.

HOW VALUE INFLUENCES CUSTOMER BUYING BEHAVIOR

The problem with measuring customer satisfaction is that it often does not predict customer buying behavior. I used to go about once a week with a group of friends to a local Italian restaurant. The food was very good, the service was good, and the prices were about average for the area. There usually was a long wait to get a table, but we would call ahead to put our name on the waiting list. We haven't been to that restaurant in over a year because another one opened nearby that is at an equal distance from my house. The new restaurant is very similar to the other one, but has much better food, is about 30 percent less expensive, and allows customers to bring their own wines. We have to wait outside for a table for sometimes as much as an hour, even though we call ahead, but it's kind of fun, because chairs are put out on the sidewalk and everyone drinks wine while waiting for a table.

We didn't switch restaurants because we were unhappy with the first one. On the contrary, we were always pleased with everything about the place. The new restaurant is just a much better value. It has better food, fine atmosphere, and the bill for dinner is less expensive. Value is always an issue; many companies don't do a good job of measuring it and linking measures of value to customer buying behavior.

DIMENSIONS OF VALUE

Up to this point, we have been talking about measuring customer satisfaction levels, which are important in determining overall value. Two other dimensions that you need to have in your scorecard are (1) perceived value and (2) price versus nearest competitors. Perceived value is a soft measure because it is a customer's opinions on the value of the product and service, for the price paid. Perceived value is a function of product and service image, as well as actual experience. Often, we perceive the price/quality ratio of a product to be acceptable until we buy that product or service and realize we may have been ripped off. For example, consider the popularity of high-end watches. The value of some of these watches is almost all in the marketing. Although the watches average between $1,000 and $2,000, they are made from either stainless steel or stainless steel and electroplated gold, and contain quartz movements, which are worth about $5. Some have sapphire crystals, which are worth a few bucks, but certainly not enough to justify the inflated price of the watch. A $2,000 watch is about $1,600 in advertising and marketing and $400 in watch. In a sense, the name is more the product than the watch itself.

Any survey you do of your customers should include at least one question about the customer's perception of the value received for the dollars spent. Perceived value is often a stronger predictor of customer buying behavior than is customer satisfaction. If you are an organization that offers multiple services and products, you might want to find out how customers perceive the value of the different products and services you offer. At a luxury hotel, I was pleased with the overall value I received for the price I paid to stay there. However, I thought the $20 per person for a fairly standard breakfast buffet was too expensive. The hotel right next door had a breakfast buffet that was comparable for $9.95. After seeing the buffet next door, I really felt cheated. Did I bother filling out a survey card in the hotel's restaurant? Nope. I simply never ate there again for breakfast. When you stay in a luxury hotel, you don't expect to find a $4 breakfast, but $20 is ridiculous even for a luxury hotel. Everyone is concerned with value, no matter how much money is being spent.

HOW VALUE PERCEPTIONS ARE DETERMINED

Value is an individual thing. People's perception of value is based on their knowledge of the cost of similar items, and what they are willing to pay for quality, prestige, rarity, and other factors that determine the price of goods and services in the marketplace. Customer satisfaction is an important determinant of future buying behavior, but not nearly as important as customers' perception of value for their dollars. Anyone who has stayed in a four-star resort, driven a Mercedes, or worn an Armani suit will usually be very happy with the quality of these products and services. However, many will never own a Mercedes, a closet full of Armani suits, or spend every vacation at a four-star resort. Value perceptions are based on our ability to afford quality products and services, what we have to sacrifice in order to afford quality, and our perceptions of whether or not the product or service is worth the money we must pay to obtain it.

In his excellent book, *Managing Customer Value*, author Bradley Gayle describes a process for determining customer value perceptions called a market-perceived quality analysis. This process involves getting customers to list the attributes of a product or service that are most important to them, and then assign a weight from 1 to 10 to each one, based on their relative importance. Bradley Gale recommends using percentages, but I like 1-to-10 ratings better because people understand this model better. For example, business executives might list the following characteristics as important to them when flying overseas in business class:

Attributes	Rating
• Large comfortable seat	8
• No smoking	10
• Amount seat reclines	3
• High quality food/drinks	5
• Choice of timing for meal service	2
• Service from flight attendants	6
• Frequent flyer program	9

Assigning importance weights to attributes is usually done in focus groups, with automated voting devices used to tabulate the importance weights assigned by individual members of the focus groups. The next step is to get customers to score or rate the performance of the company being evaluated against one or two of their major competitors. For example, United Airlines might ask its customers to rate their performance and American Airlines' performance on each of these attributes on a 1-to-10 scale. By multiplying the ratings by the weights, each company receives an overall score for value performance. The one with the higher score will theoretically be the one that gets selected by the customer. A hypothetical example is presented below:

Competitive Value Analysis

Attribute	Weight	UNITED		AMERICAN	
		Rating	Total	Rating	Total
Seat Comfort	8	8	64	9	72
No Smoking	10	10	100	10	100
Reclining Seat	3	4	12	5	15
Food/Drink	5	8	40	6	30
Meal Timing	2	10	20	2	4
Service Level	6	6	36	8	48
Frequent Flyer Prog.	9	7	63	8	72
Totals			335		341

In this example there is no clear winner. Both companies end up with about the same scores, so it may be other factors like price and schedule that determine which airline the customer will select.

The problem with this type of research is that it assumes that customers go through a logical thought process when making a purchase. Many people make major buying decisions on impulse, without going through much logical analysis. A friend of mine recently decided to buy a new Porsche 911, after considering an Acura NSX and a Dodge Viper. When asked why he bought a 911, he said that it looked the coolest of the three cars. On this guy's list of important car attributes, he probably has one item that was given a weight of 100%; cool-looking styling. I doubt that it would have turned out that way if he participated in a focus group, however. My point is that you have to be careful with doing research on customer perceptions, because what people tell you is important to them in a focus group may not be what actually controls their buying behavior. Market research is far from an exact science, because people are not very good observers of their own behavior and feelings.

PRICE VERSUS COMPETITION: THE HARD MEASURE OF VALUE

Just as your customer satisfaction metrics should include hard measures of actual buying behavior, you need to have some hard measures of value. The most important one is how your prices compare to those of your nearest competitors. Comparing prices is actually how many customers determine how they feel about value. During my first morning at a luxury hotel in Hawaii, I just assumed that most of the big hotels charged $20 for breakfast, so I accepted it, even though I felt that it was expensive, even by comparing it to the cost of breakfast in hotels in Manhattan. However, when I found out that the competition next door had about the same breakfast buffet for half the price, I really felt cheated. Perhaps this hotel knew what its competition was charging and didn't care, or perhaps it is arrogant enough to believe that, with its quality and reputation, it has no competition.

All organizations need to measure their prices versus those of their competitors as often as possible. The airlines measure this on a daily basis because they know that price drives customers' buying behavior in a big way. Car rental companies monitor competitors' prices, but their business does not seem to be quite as sensitive to price as the airlines. AT&T, which I believe is the benchmark when it comes to measuring customer satisfaction and value, has narrowed down its customer value-added metrics:

- Price competitiveness.

- Customer value perception.

- Customer satisfaction.

In measuring customer perceptions regarding value, AT&T looks at three dimensions:

1. Overall value: service was worth the price.

2. Relative perceived quality: service quality versus competitors' quality.

3. Relative price: price satisfaction versus competitors' price.

LINKING CUSTOMER VALUE TO THE CUSTOMER SATISFACTION INDEX

One approach is to have two overall metrics in the customer section of your scorecard: a customer satisfaction index (CSI), which includes hard

TABLE 6.3   Example of Customer Value Index (CVI)

Metric	Importance Weight
Survey scores	30%
Overall value (15%)	
Price vs. competitors' (15%)	
Focus group scores	30%
Overall value (10%)	
Product quality/price (5%)	
Service quality/price (5%)	
Our value vs. competitors' (10%)	
Actual price versus competitors'	40%
Product A (15%)	
Product B (10%)	
Product C (15%)	

and soft measures of customer satisfaction, and a customer value index (CVI). The CVI should consist of soft or opinion measures, collected via surveys and focus groups, such as customer perception of the value versus the price and customers' perception of your prices versus competitors'. The CVI should also include at least one hard measure of your prices versus those of your nearest competitors. The overall CVI measure might be made up of the statistics shown in Table 6.3. Just like a CSI, the CVI should be computed on a 100-point scale, so that data analysis and interpretation are made easy.

Another approach is to combine the CSI and the CVI into a single index of overall satisfaction and value. This is how AT&T does it. AT&T has one statistic in its scorecard called "Customer Value-Added" that is a combination of hard and soft data on customer satisfaction, value perception, and actual prices versus competitors'. The overall weight given to the value component of the equation versus the satisfaction portion varies, depending upon the importance of price and value versus quality in the customers' buying decisions. For example, in the long-distance business, price and value are extremely important, because customers perceive that there is little difference in quality from one long-distance carrier to another. In AT&T's credit card business, Universal Card Systems, value is not as much of an issue because AT&T charges no annual fee to most of its customers and interest rates are about average for the industry. Customers use the AT&T card the most and stay with AT&T because of service and convenience, rather than price/value. Consequently, the weight given the CSI component in the scorecard for the credit card business is higher.

Whether you decide to measure value and pricing as part of your overall CSI or to keep it separate, it is crucial that you don't exclude it. According to author Bradley Gale, AT&T found that there was no direct correlation between customer satisfaction scores and market share or customer buying behavior. In fact, AT&T was losing market share even though satisfaction ratings consistently hovered around 90 percent. Only after it started measuring value along with satisfaction did customers' buying behavior show a correlation with ratings. For additional information on measuring and linking customer satisfaction and value, I highly recommend *Managing Customer Value* by Bradley T. Gale (New York: The Free Press, 1994). This book is the most practical and well-researched text I've seen on linking customer satisfaction and value analysis to key business metrics.

HOW EXCELLENT ORGANIZATIONS MEASURE CUSTOMER SATISFACTION AND VALUE

- Customers are segmented according to similar characteristics and their specific needs are determined at least once a year.

- Specific surveys are developed to measure satisfaction levels of each group of customers.

- Large samples of customers are surveyed at least twice a year, and a large percentage (for example, 50 percent or more) of the surveys are answered.

- The organization conducts focus groups or similar meetings with various groups of customers several times each year to gather qualitative customer satisfaction data.

- Customer satisfaction telephone and mail surveys are evaluated and continually improved.

- Hard data such as repeat business are collected to supplement data on customers' opinions of the organization's products/services.

- Individual indices of customer satisfaction are summarized into a customer satisfaction index (CSI).

- Customer satisfaction levels of key competitors are determined.

- Internal support functions all have simple but thorough methods for determining the satisfaction levels of their customers.

- A variety of hard and soft (opinion) data are collected on customer value.

- Price and quality data on key competitors are collected on a regular basis to assess value performance.

Measuring Product/Service Quality

This is the section on your scorecard where you plot key quality variables relating to the products you manufacture or the services you sell. This is not customer satisfaction data, although the two are certainly related. In this box on your scoreboard, you put your measure of your quality. These are the data from tests, inspections, and various measurements of your performance. In this chapter, I will explain some of the mistakes organizations make when measuring the quality of their products and services and provide some suggestions on how to select the most appropriate measures.

PRODUCTS, SERVICES, OR BOTH?

In a manufacturing company, it's very easy to identify what the products are. Manufacturing companies are almost always in the service business as well. Black & Decker not only sells drills, and other tools and equipment, it sells repair services, delivery, marketing assistance for retailers, and a number of services. Service organizations do not necessarily have products, however. McDonald's sells both products and service. The food is the product and the services are cooking the food, serving it, providing a clean place to eat, a playground for the kids, a bathroom, and so on. A bank does not sell any products. Banks won't agree with this, but a loan or a CD is not a product. The bank does not manufacture a product as McDonald's does in preparing an order of french fries. Does a school have products? Smarter students perhaps? No, a school or university is a service organization, as is a healthcare organization.

CUSTOMER REQUIREMENTS DRIVE PRODUCT/SERVICE QUALITY MEASURES

In the previous chapter, I talked a lot about how important it is to find out what is really important to your customers about each of your products and services. This information on what customers want and expect also helps tell you what dimensions of your products or services need to be measured and controlled. Because what customers want and expect changes quite often, it is important to conduct customer requirements research on a regular and frequent basis. Some of the leading companies today use customer requirements to drive the new product design process. Using an approach called quality function deployment, firms like Mazda and Hewlett-Packard define specific customer requirements for products that don't yet exist. These use these customer "wish lists" to drive the design process, so that they eventually come out with products that people want to buy. The new Cadillac Seville with the Northstar engine that goes 100,000 miles between tune-ups is another example of a product that was designed around customer requirements.

ATTENTION TO DETAIL

Go into any successful service business. McDonald's, Ritz-Carlton, Walt Disney, Citicorp, and most other highly rated service organizations have a very simple formula for their success: *attention to detail.* Nothing is left to chance. Every aspect of the service is measured and controlled so that the customer gets consistently excellent service and value for the money. Ritz-Carlton measures over 600 individual metrics related to the various services they offer to guests. Each is based upon hundreds of focus groups and other types of data-gathering techniques to find out what is most important to customers who stay at luxury hotels. In fact, Ritz-Carlton has also built a database of the unique needs of each of its customers. If you stay at the Ritz-Carlton in Boston and request a nonallergenic face soap and a nonfeather pillow, you will not only receive these items promptly, but the next time you check into a Ritz-Carlton anywhere in the world, these items will be in your room! Using its extensive database of customer needs, Ritz-Carlton can tailor its services to each customer. The key in making this attention-to-detail formula work is to make sure you are paying attention to the right details. Emphasize the things that really matter to customers rather than the things that are easy to measure and control.

QUALITY GARBAGE

It seems very easy to make money in the sanitation business. However, it's more complicated than it might seem to an outsider. Picking up people's garbage is a fairly low-tech service business, and customers have some very basic requirements that need to be met. Browning-Ferris Industries (BFI), one of the largest sanitation companies, used to measure service quality with one simple metric: whether the trash was picked up on the appropriate day each week for every customer location. The company historically lost about 15 percent of its customer base each year to large competitors like Waste Management. In fact, it was losing about 4,000 to 5,000 customers per month, and only gaining about 6,000. For every three steps forward, it took two steps back. The reason for this turnover or "churn" of customers was always thought to be price. Competitors come in and offer a slightly lower price for garbage collection and the customer switches. Sanitation is a commodity service right? It turned out that price was not the reason customers were leaving—it was service. In doing some customer requirements research, BFI found out that customers have a fairly long list of requirements for their sanitation service. They are:

- Timeliness.
- Quiet trucks.
- Cans/dumpsters returned to original locations.
- Cans/dumpsters undamaged.
- No debris/garbage left in cans/dumpsters.
- Reasonable fees.
- All garbage collected.
- Quiet garbage collectors.
- Timely invoices sent quarterly.

Once BFI determined that customers wanted much more than their garbage picked up every Tuesday morning, it began measuring many aspects of its service that it had never previously measured. Quality inspectors periodically checked to make sure that the requirements customers had expressed were actually being met. BFI also began surveying its customers to find out what they thought of the service. The combination of its own service quality measures and customer feedback gave a good picture of performance. So, if it did this in 1988, what has happened since then? Well, it still loses some customers every month, but nowhere near as many as it used to, and it consistently rates the same or slightly better in customer satisfaction and service quality as its biggest competitor, Waste Management.

BREAKING DOWN PRODUCTS AND SERVICES
AND IDENTIFYING MEASURES

Every organization has multiple products and services, so each needs to have its own quality dimensions and measures identified. A complicated product like an airplane or a car may have many different components or subsystems, each having its own set of product quality dimensions and measures to be identified. Even a simple product like a tube of toothpaste may require a breakdown into measures that relate to the packaging, the tube, and the toothpaste itself. Each may have its own measures of quality. A service organization needs to break down its specific services in a similar manner and define measures that may be unique to individual services (see Table 7.1). Each individual product or service may have many different attributes or characteristics that need to be measured. The difficulty lies in measuring all the important characteristics and in not measuring irrelevant factors.

QUALITY IS NOT JUST GOODNESS

Quality is usually thought to be accuracy or the absence of defects. A quality car is one that has no problems, runs, and works all the time. Quality is much broader than an absence of defects. Although accuracy and an absence of defects are important with most products and services, other dimensions of quality are sometimes equally or even more important. Quality can include measures of

- Accuracy.
- Completeness.
- Conformance.

TABLE 7.1   Hierarchy of Services—Hotel Example

Service Functions
- Guest services
- Reservations/sales
- Banquets/food/beverages
- Facilities

Service Groupings
- Bellman
- Concierge
- Operator
- Housekeeping

Individual Services
- Wake-up calls
- Calling assistance
- Messages

Quality Measures
- Guest called on time
- Use guest name when taking request

- Innovation/novelty.
- Class.

Accuracy is probably the best understood and most common type of quality measure. It is certainly important in a medical laboratory or just about any healthcare service, a bank, an airline, and any organization where precision is important. Completeness is another dimension of quality that is fairly common. Whether all required fields on a computer screen are filled might be a measure of completeness. Or whether the construction contractor completed all checklist items identified during a walk-through. Conformance is another measure of quality. It has to do with how well the product or service meets specifications or standards. Some conformance measures include the following:

- How well the tile installation matches the architect's design drawings.

- How well the machine setup stays within the standards set for that particular job.

- The extent to which the proposal follows the style and sequence standards set for the company's sales proposals.

Conformance to standards has to do with the extent to which a product or service looks the way it is supposed to look and performs the way it is supposed to perform.

Innovation or novelty is another type of quality dimension that is very important for some types of products and services. When flying in a Boeing 747, you don't want the pilot to get creative when it comes time to land the plane. There is a specific landing procedure that must be followed with precision every single time. However, with other jobs, creativity is the important dimension of quality—not necessarily accuracy or completeness. A print ad for a new shampoo and a car are examples. The difference between a high-quality and a low-quality advertisement has nothing to do with accuracy or completeness, or following established standards for print ads. Creativity and novelty are what we pay an advertising agency for. How about software design? That is another product where creativity is highly desired. Or how about the movie business? What determines a box office success versus a failure are dimensions such as creativity, action, likable characters, good story line, and so on. Films that are derived from novels are seldom complete, and often not accurate when it comes to following the sequence of events in the book. Accuracy and completeness are not important quality dimensions for a film.

The final dimension of quality is called "class." Class has to do with aesthetics, appearance, use ability, and so on. It is related to creativity, but not the same thing. Class is an important quality dimension in any product or service trying to appeal to the buyer on an emotional level. For those of you who remember the 1970s, recall the American Motors Pacer, clearly a unique and creative car design. It was also one of the ugliest and was not a best-selling model. Later in the decade (1978–1979), Cadillac came out with its new Seville, with the bustle-back styling borrowed from the Rolls Royces of the 1930s. Perhaps not as creative a design as the Pacer, which looked like no other car, the Seville, however, could certainly be said to have more style and class. In fact, the Seville of that era is considered by many to be one of the best-looking cars Cadillac ever made.

Dimensions of quality such as class or creativity cannot be measured with complete objectivity. Good writing, good film, good graphic design, and a number of other important accomplishments are impossible to measure objectively. Ten individuals will rarely agree on ratings for dimensions like creativity and class. However, if these are what are important, they need to at least be measured subjectively, with some attempt to remove some of the variability from the measurement system.

QUANTITY AND QUALITY MEASURES

If you work in a manufacturing company, the quantity, or number, of units you produce is almost as important a measure as the quality of the products. In the garment industry, for example, workers are still paid on a piece-rate system, where their pay is based on the number of units they sew that pass quality inspections. The amount of work that is completed is also important in service organizations, such as the number of patients processed per hour in a hospital emergency room, the number of phone calls handled per hour by a customer service department, and so forth. Quantity measures of work completed go in this section of your organization's scorecard because they are an output measure. Measures of quantity of work completed per employee or other measures of productivity go in the section of your measurement report that addresses process data, which is described in the next chapter.

ESTABLISHING A PRODUCT/SERVICE QUALITY INDEX

Imagine that you are the general manager of a product division or brand manager in a product line that contains 18 different products. Are you going to want to review detailed product quality data on each individual product every week? I doubt it. Every organization needs detailed measures of individual service and product quality. This may mean that it has hundreds or even thousands of measures in its product/service quality database. However, at some point these data need to be aggregated so that the leaders can get a feel for product/service quality levels without getting into the details of hundreds of pages of data.

What some organizations do is put together a product or service quality report card that summarizes key product or service quality data. Each dimension of the product or service is given a weight, based on the relative importance of that dimension to the customer. Each product or ser-

TABLE 7.2   Sample Administrative Services Product Report Card

Products/Services	Weight	Score	Weighted Score
Printing/reproduction	20%	72%	14.4
Overhead transparencies	15%	84%	12.6
Slides	15%	77%	11.6
Word processing services	30%	71%	21.3
Graphics services	10%	85%	8.5
Delivery services	10%	59%	5.9
Total score for month			74.3/100
Goal: 80%	YTD average: 76.2%	Last year June: 67.8%	

vice is then given a weight based on its sales or importance, to provide a measure of overall service quality. Table 7.2 shows an example of how a report card might look for an administrative service organization.

If you are the manager of the Administrative Services department, this is all you need to look at each month to tell you about your product and service quality. This report card shows that the department has failed to meet its goal of 80/100, but is quite a bit better in performance than during June of the previous year. The report card also tells the manager that delivery services appear to be a problem and that word processing did not score very well either. The manager could then ask to see individual report cards for delivery services and for word processing. Each of these report cards would include a breakdown of the individual measures of performance for these services. An example of the report card for word processing services is shown in Table 7.3.

A separate report card is prepared once a month in this Administrative Services area for each of its major products and services. These individual report cards are then summarized into an overall summary for the department. The manager of the Word Processing function gets the detailed report card on word processing, and his manager, the leader of Administrative Services, sees only the department product/service report card. The weights of each of the product/service quality dimensions are established by the customers of the word processing services, not by the department itself. Notice that timeliness, getting the word processing completed by the deadline, is considered to be the most important measure. This system of putting together a product/service

TABLE 7.3 Sample Word Processing Report Card

Measure	Weight	Score	Weighted Score
Accuracy (no defects)	20%	64%	12.8
Completeness	20%	77%	15.4
Timeliness	25%	82%	20.5
Format guidelines followed	10%	70%	7
Aesthetics/layout	10%	56%	5.6
Consistency	15%	62%	9.3
Total score for month			70.6/100
Goal: 85%	YTD: 68.7%	Last year June: 66.5%	

score allows you to set it up in whatever way makes the most sense for your organization. Organizations often change their product scorecard as certain measures of product/service quality change in their importance. For example, word processing may decide to make accuracy the most important factor, because many reports are completed on time, but with numerous errors.

The product report card concept can apply to everyone from an individual hourly employee up to the chief executive of the organization. The CEO or the head of a division or business unit would look at an overall report card for all products/services. Consider an example. Schmedrick, Falchar, and Wanermeyer is one of the oldest and largest public accounting and management consulting firms in the country. The company has no products. It divides its business according to three major service lines: (1) auditing, (2) taxes, and (3) consulting.

The partner in charge of each of these three business units receives a monthly report card. The consulting practice involves a wide variety of projects, ranging from multimillion dollar fixed-fee engagements to design a new system or help the client company install a new initiative such as activity-based costing (ABC) or reengineering, to ongoing pure consulting work. The ongoing consulting projects are billed by the hour or day and produce no clear outputs or products. The quality dimensions that are important for the fixed-fee projects with clear deliverables are shown in Table 7.4.

Some of the measures from the previous example are clear and others require some explanation. For example, the *client relationship index* is a

TABLE 7.4   Measurements for Fixed-Fee Projects

Measure	Weight	Score	Weighted Score
Percentage of deadlines met	20%	96%	19.2
Client relationship index	25%	84%	21
Use of established methodology	10%	100%	10
Innovation index	15%	68%	10.2
Solution design quality	20%	76%	15.2
Report format/quality	10%	94%	9.4
Total			85/100
Goal: 90% (all areas)	YTD: 86.4%	Last April: 81%	

measure of how well the consultants respond to client phone calls, demonstrate a knowledge of the client's business, exhibit flexibility in dealings with clients, frequency of client contact, and the level of contact with the individuals in the client's firm. Each of the six separate measures in the consulting services report card has its own measurement instruments that are used to collect and summarize the data on a sample of all consulting projects being worked on at any given time. Sampling is used because the organization does not have the time or resources to evaluate each of the hundreds of consulting engagements every month. A report card similar to the one shown in Table 7.4 is also prepared for the hourly consulting projects where there is no deliverable. These projects account for less than 20 percent of the firm's consulting income, so they are given a much lower weight in the overall report card for consulting services. The summary sheet that the managing partner looks at might be as simple as the one in Table 7.5.

The example shows that the consulting services practice is slightly below the goal of 90 percent for April. If the practice manager wanted to find out why, he would refer to the report card for the fixed-fee projects and determine where the problem is. By reviewing the fixed-fee report card, that manager learns that three areas are below goal:

- Innovation index   68
- Solution design quality   76
- Client relationship index 84

TABLE 7.5   Sample Summary Sheet

Project Type	Score	Weight	Weighted Score
Fixed fee	85%	80%	68
Hourly rate	94%	20%	18.8
Total consulting services score			86.8
Goal: 90% YTD score: 87.4% Last April: 82.3%			

By asking for a further breakdown of the data, the manager can determine if the low scores on these three measures are coming from a particular type of project, or perhaps from a particular group of consultants. If the overall service quality index showed performance to be above the goal of 90 percent, the managing partner would not need to see the detail.

HOW EXCELLENT ORGANIZATIONS MEASURE PRODUCT/SERVICE QUALITY

- Quality measurement dimensions are defined based upon factors that will delight customers.

- Collect data on sufficiently large samples of products/services.

- Assign an importance weight to each quality dimension, based upon the relative importance of each to customers.

- Summarize product/service quality data into aggregate indices such as an overall quality index.

- Set standards for product/service quality levels based on customer requirements and quality levels of world-class organizations' products/services.

- Use objective third-party product/service quality data to supplement internal data.

Measuring Processes and Operational Performance

THE KEY TO EXCELLENCE

The key to excellence in any organization is control of its processes to produce reliable and consistent products and services. Performing the right processes in the right manner leads to consistent levels of product and service quality. The difficulty lies in finding the right process variables to measure and setting the standards appropriate to performance levels of each of the process measures. Process and operational measures are leading-edge measures that are more short-term-focused. These are the measures that are typically monitored every day or at least every week. Some process variables are even monitored continuously to ensure the production and delivery of high-quality products and services. Achieving good performance levels on process or operational measures leads to high-quality products and services, which, in turn, lead to satisfied or delighted customers, which lead to repeat business and promote your organization's long-term survival and success. Figure 8.1 depicts this graphically.

In order to achieve consistently high performance, an organization must control its inputs. The two most important inputs to good performance are knowledge of customer requirements and high-quality goods and services from key suppliers.

WHY MEASURE PROCESSES?

Organizations care about results much more than how those results are achieved. If an executive is running a business unit that is achieving unheard-of profits using some nontraditional approaches, who cares? If a salesman is outselling his peers by 35 percent but isn't thought to be a

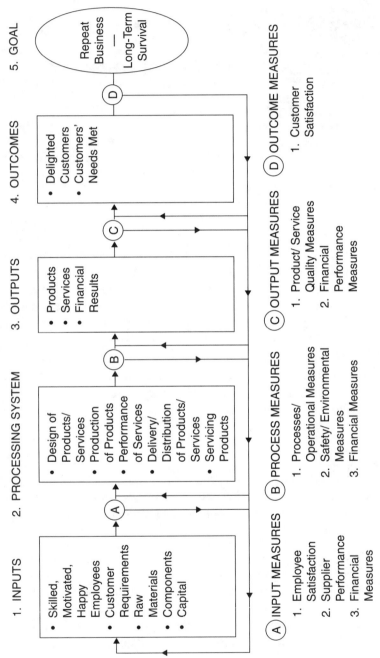

FIGURE 8.1 Macro Process Model of an Organization

1. INPUTS

- Skilled, Motivated, Happy Employees
- Customer Requirements
- Raw Materials
- Components
- Capital

2. PROCESSING SYSTEM

- Design of Products/ Services
- Production of Products
- Performance of Services
- Delivery/ Distribution of Products/ Services
- Servicing Products

3. OUTPUTS

- Products
- Services
- Financial Results

4. OUTCOMES

- Delighted Customers
- Customers' Needs Met

5. GOAL

Repeat Business — Long-Term Survival

Ⓐ INPUT MEASURES

1. Employee Satisfaction
2. Supplier Performance
3. Financial Measures

Ⓑ PROCESS MEASURES

1. Processes/ Operational Measures
2. Safety/ Environmental Measures
3. Financial Measures

Ⓒ OUTPUT MEASURES

1. Product/ Service Quality Measures
2. Financial Performance Measures

Ⓓ OUTCOME MEASURES

1. Customer Satisfaction

team player, who cares? Shouldn't an organization focus on outputs and results rather than processes? Won't focusing on activity or process measures lead to the wrong performance? The answer to all of these questions is that you always care about how results or outputs are achieved. Process measures provide you with the data needed to predict and control the quality of your products and services. When a problem occurs with a product or service, the cause is usually found by looking at the process data. Results and outcomes are important for all organizations. In fact, they may be the most important thing. But how those results are achieved—the process measures—is also very important to track.

PROCESS VERSUS OUTPUT MEASURES

Process measures are measures of activity or behavior; they are not measures of outputs or of suboutputs. In a hotel's housekeeping department, a process measure might be the use of the appropriate cleanser to clean the bathtub. An output measure might be whether or not the bathtub meets cleanliness standards. People often confuse measures of suboutputs with process measures. Managers at a large bakery told me their process measures for various stages in the baking process were viscosity of the batter/dough, sweetness of the batter, the uniformity of the sizes of the loaves as they are divided for baking, the volume and weight of each cake or loaf of bread before and after baking, color, taste, and so on. None of these is a process measure. These are measures of suboutputs and belong in the section of your scorecard that deals with product/service quality. Checking the viscosity of the cake batter is a product quality measure. Process variables that should be measured in a bakery might include the following:

- Use of the appropriate quantities of ingredients.
- Speed of the mixer.
- Length of time the batter/dough is mixed.
- Temperature of the oven.
- Amount of time the dough is given to rise.

The logic behind process measures is that if you control all of your processes, you will get the same outputs every single time if you have good raw materials. At Zenith, the last American company to produce televisions, not one of the TVs is taken into a lab to test it. The company relies almost exclusively on process data to tell it about the consistency of product quality. Zenith has done enough research and has sufficiently tight control strategies in place to avoid having to do any final inspection of the products. It knows that the televisions will work from looking at process data.

If you go into an Alcoa plant, where aluminum is made that is used to manufacture beer and soft drink cans, you see almost no people. These plants are longer than several football fields and are run almost by remote control. Alcoa, like Zenith, does very little testing of the quality of the final product. It controls all key process variables so that consistent quality is produced on every single roll that comes out of the plants.

HOW TO SELECT THE RIGHT PROCESS MEASURES

Selecting the right process measures is relatively easy if you have thoroughly defined customer requirements and have done research to identify the specific process variables that are correlated with product or service characteristics that customers care about. For example, one of Alcoa's large customers is Coors Beer. It buys rolled aluminum from Alcoa that is used to manufacture beer cans. Along with price, two of Coors' most important requirements about the aluminum is its strength and its thickness. The aluminum has to be extremely thin so that it is light and inexpensive. It also has to be strong enough to stand up as a rigid beverage can. One of Alcoa's key processes is rolling. During the rolling process, the pretreated aluminum ingot is under thousands of pounds of pressure until it eventually becomes thin enough to make a beer can. A key process measure is temperature. Do you think Coors or other Alcoa customers care about the temperature of the aluminum when it arrives at their dock? I guarantee you they do not. If it's hot outside, the aluminum is hot, and if it's cold, so is the aluminum. Alcoa measures temperature because it is a process variable that is highly correlated with product characteristics that customers do care about: strength and thickness. Alcoa learned about the importance of controlling temperature through research and experience.

The same sort of research that Alcoa and others do has to go into the selection of appropriate process variables to measure in your organization. Rarely have I seen an organization that has a good set of process measures. Most are based on superstition and tradition. By superstition, I mean that someone believes that the measure is correlated with success based on experience rather than being based on research and hard objective data. For example, one of the first acts that an executive took after taking control a large business unit in one of the Fortune 500 manufacturing companies was to cancel casual Fridays. He believed that casual dress led to casual attitudes and was related to sloppy work; employees were just too relaxed. So the suits and the skirts came back after the organization had had casual Fridays for more than five years. A good way to make a positive impression on the troops, right? I asked this executive if he could cite any research that indicated that suits and skirts were somehow related to employee productivity, safety, or any other important performance measure. He couldn't think of any, but in his experience, employees were just more professional when they were dressed as professionals. Although the company did not actually measure the percentage of employees who dress professionally, this is a perfect example of how a process variable or practice is selected based on superstition.

Tradition is often the other main reason why process measures are selected. Look out when you hear the phrase: "We've always tracked the number of _____." The key to having a good database for any organization is simplicity. That means screening out all the extraneous data that do not really need to be collected and reviewed.

ORGANIZATIONS THAT DEPEND ON PEOPLE

In some manufacturing organizations, very little of what they do is controlled by employees. Labor may account for less than 5 percent of the total manufacturing cost. Process control is achieved through automation. Using technology to monitor and control key process variables is a great way of ensuring consistent product quality. In organizations that depend a great deal on human behavior to get their work done, process measures and controls are much more difficult to come up with. Aircraft manufacturer Northrop Grumman, for example, depends a great deal on the behavior of its employees to achieve results. If you walk through a Northrop Grumman plant, you will see thousands of people doing things with their hands. Similarly, a hospital, a government agency, a school, and most service businesses rely on employees to perform most key processes. When this is the case, it becomes difficult to come up with good process measures that will drive the right behaviors.

A military organization I worked with cared about the health and fitness of its personnel. One of the process variables for which it collected data was hours spent in the gym per month per person. Because each individual had to sign in and out, it was something that was easy to track, and hard to fake. However, it drove the wrong behavior. What many would do is sign in at the gym and go sit in the whirlpool or the snack bar, socializing for an hour or two, 2 or 3 days a week. Spending time in the gym does not mean that the time will be spent exercising. Gyms and health clubs have become a place to socialize as much as they are a place to get fit.

The key to good behavioral process measures is to do the research to determine the impact that performance of the behavior will have on product/service quality and on customer satisfaction levels. For example, McDonald's and many other service companies measure the smiles that their customer contact employees give customers. Counting smiles is a process measure. However, a smile from an employee has been found through research to have a major impact on the customer's satisfaction levels with the service. Don't make the mistake of guessing or assuming that certain behaviors will lead to certain results. Recall the story of the "Have a nice day" campaign from Chapter 2.

AVOID FOOLISHLY COPYING COMPETITORS' PROCESS MEASURES

Whenever one organization tries to add a little something extra to its products or services to help distinguish it from competitors, you can bet that that practice will be copied by competitors and that they will begin collecting data on that measure. Remember the days when hotels never folded the ends of the toilet paper into a nice neat arrow so that it was easy to grab? One started doing it and now they all do. Even when we check into Motel 6 for $22 a night, we expect that it will at least fold the corners of the toilet paper rolls for us. Or how about the two chocolates on the pillow and bed turn-down service? Remember when only a few expensive hotels did this? Then they all started doing it, until they found out how much that little extra cost them. Now they put a card by the bed and tell you to call if you want the turn-down service. No chocolates anymore, though, unless you're paying $200 a night.

Foolishly copying a competitor often leads to wasted money and time, and the collection of data on a behavior of your employees that customers don't really care about any way. Better to spend money and time researching those behaviors and process measures that are correlated with quality, financial results, and customer satisfaction.

CYCLE TIME

One type of process measure that should be part of any organization's scorecard is total cycle time. Total cycle time, or simply cycle time, is the amount of time that elapses between an input or stimulus and the completion of a task. For example, Domino's Pizza measures the cycle time between when a customer order is taken and when the pizza is delivered to the customer. Domino's made a name by being the only pizza company that could get a pizza delivered in 30 minutes or less. Time is a critical process measure for any task because it equates to cost and satisfying customers' needs. Customers want things quickly and they don't want to pay a lot of money. Focusing on cycle time allows an organization to keep its costs down while satisfying or even delighting customers. Philip Thomas even goes so far as to suggest that measuring cycle time is the key to an organization's competitiveness. In his book, *Competitiveness Through Total Cycle Time* (New York: McGraw-Hill, 1990), Thomas makes a case for cycle time being as important as financial measures to evaluate an organization's performance.

Cycle time should be measured in all support areas as well as in the production/service delivery functions of the organization. In fact, cycle time is most often a problem with support areas. Think about the law department in a big corporation as an example. The most frequent complaint about the law department is how long it takes to review documents. Or how about the MIS department and how long it takes to develop or modify software that is requested by internal customers. Cycle time is also often a problem in government organizations. How long did you stand in line the last time you went to the DMV? Have you recently applied for a mortgage? Gathering the data needed to review and approve or deny a mortgage actually takes less than a couple of hours. Yet it is common to wait 30 days to get a mortgage approved. Opportunities for improving cycle time by huge proportions can be found in all types of organizations. Cycle time is not only important from an internal efficiency and cost standpoint, it is almost always one of the things customers care about.

You have to be careful when coming up with the actual measure of cycle time so that you gather the appropriate data. The definition of cycle time should be the entire time that elapses between when a customer need is expressed and when it is eventually satisfied. Customers won't be too impressed if the cycle time for evaluating the eligibility of a claim for payment is reduced unless overall claims processing time has been reduced. Companies and sometimes entire industries play games with cycle time numbers to make themselves look good. Once airlines began being tracked for their on-time performance, they changed their definition of on-time performance. An on-time takeoff is defined as the time the plane pushes away from the jetway. If the plane sits on the runway for an hour before taking off, it is still considered an on-time takeoff. On-time landings are also tracked, and these data are faulty as well. As soon as the airlines started being evaluated on this measure, they padded their schedules by 15 to 30 minutes to help ensure that their on-time performance looks good. For example, a flight from Los Angeles to San Francisco is about 45 to 55 minutes, but the scheduled time for the flight is an hour and 20 minutes.

EMPLOYEE PRODUCTIVITY

Productivity was the measurement *du jour* of the 1980s. I was a productivity improvement consultant in the 1980s. The American Productivity Center in Houston was formed back in those days. You may have noticed that it changed its name to the American Productivity and *Quality* Center about five years ago when productivity fell out of favor and was replaced by the quality movement. I had to change my business cards to tell potential clients that I was now a *quality consultant.* Since 1995, quality has had a bad reputation. Even the Malcolm Baldrige National Quality Award has removed most of the reference to quality from its 1995 criteria. So what happened to productivity? It's still around and it still has to be measured. No one measure by itself gives a complete picture of organizational health, whether it's quality, cycle time, or productivity. Data on all of these measures must be looked at when evaluating organizational performance.

All organizations need to have some productivity indices in their scorecard to help tell them if their human and nonhuman resources are being used wisely. Productivity measures are always a ratio of some sort of output or accomplishment to some measure of resources. Typically, the resources have to do with people, but not always. Some common productivity measures in organizations are as follows:

- Flights per day.

- Dollars in sales per employee.

- Dollars in profits per employee.

- Number of units produced per employee.

- Number of units divided by labor costs.

- Energy costs divided by production.

- Number of units of good quality produced divided by raw material costs.

Productivity measures tell us whether we're getting our money's worth from our people and other inputs to the organization. The difficult part about productivity measures is selecting the right variables and selecting the correct standards or goals. In Chapter 3, I talked about measuring writers based on how many pages they write per day, or measuring researchers in a corporate R&D function on how many papers they publish per year. Both of these are measures of productivity that drive the wrong performance.

Macro measures of productivity for an entire organization are usually fairly good. Indices like sales per employee are important and useful in evaluating organizational performance. It's once you get down to the department or individual job level that productivity measures tend to become stupid. The key to selecting the right productivity measures throughout the organization is to ask whether the output being measured (the top half of the productivity ratio) is of value to the organization's customers. In the case of writers, pages are certainly a valuable output to the customers of the writers. In the case of articles published in journals by researchers, I don't think that R&D's customers even care about journal articles. A second point is to be sure that the measure of outputs is the appropriate index. Number of pages per day is not what is important. Number of good pages per day is what the customers of the writers are looking for.

SAFETY METRICS

Just about all manufacturing and many service organizations need to have good safety metrics. Safety impacts employee morale, productivity, and overall financial results. A good set of safety metrics includes some that are of outputs and some that are more preventive in nature. The typical manufacturing organization measures things like number of lost-time accidents, the number of accidents, and the dollars spent in worker compensation costs. Whereas these are good output measures, they do nothing to help prevent safety problems. Measuring lost-time accidents is like measuring quality by counting rejects or defects. A good safety index includes both preventive and output measures.

Controlling safety boils down to controlling employee behavior in the workplace. Safety training and a few posters are hardly enough to control much behavior on a daily basis. The nuclear industry does a fairly thorough job of measuring safety because it track all sorts of process metrics, such as safety audits, training and retraining, and behavioral measures such as evidence of unsafe practices. A good overall safety index contains several output metrics like number of lost-time accidents and several behavioral or preventive measures such as safety audit scores or near misses.

OTHER COMMON PROCESS MEASURES

Along with productivity, cycle time, and safety, another common process measure used in manufacturing and service organizations is scrap or yield. This is certainly an important measure for a paper company, or almost any manufacturing organization. Yield is actually a measure of the productivity of raw materials usage. For example, in the clothing industry, they measure designers and cutters based on how much scrap fabric is left over after a garment's piece parts have been cut. Along with labor, fabric cost is one of the most expensive parts of the garment, so it is important that patterns are laid out to allow for the least amount of scrap possible before the fabric is cut. Scrap or yield is also an important measure in the restaurant business. Spoilage and food that is cooked and not sold costs restaurants a great deal and can dramatically impact profitability.

Another common process measure that is appropriate for many types of organizations is rework. Rework is time spent fixing a product or service that was not done right the first time. I heard a speech from a Mercedes Benz executive several year ago in Frankfurt. He talked about the exceptional quality of cars that Mercedes manufactures—a point no one would argue. However, he explained that one of Mercedes' biggest challenges was to reduce the amount of rework that goes into each car. He suggested that the amount of labor and material that go to rework on a typical Mercedes car is enough to build an entire medium-price car from scratch. In other words, there is about $15,000 worth of rework in a typical $85,000 Mercedes. One way of measuring rework is to calculate what Phil Crosby calls the *cost of quality*. Whether rework is measured in dollars, hours, or some other index, it is of critical importance for most organizations.

DEVELOPING A PROCESS REPORT CARD: PLOTTING THE BIG FOUR

As with the other major sections in your organization's scorecard, I recommend limiting your data to a few key process variables and summarizing process data into a single index if possible. All organizations, from a major corporation to a small department in a public organization, need to have data on productivity, cycle time, safety, and rework. These are the big four of the process measures, and they cut across all types and sizes of organizations. In fact, if these were the only four macro process measures for which you collect data, you might be fine. Of course, you will need a number of subsidiary process metrics to control all key processes in your organization, but here we're only talking about the highest level of measures. As in the other chapters, I recommend assigning a weight to each of the process variables/measures based on its importance. An example of a process report card for any type of organization is shown in Table 8.1.

It all looks so simple, right? The difficult part is converting the raw data to scores of 100, 1,000, or some other nice round number. In order to

TABLE 8.1   Example of Process Report Card

Measurement Index	Weight	Score	Weighted Score	Goal
Productivity	20%	80%	16	18
Cycle time	25%	86%	21.5	21
Safety index	15%	100%	15	15
Rework index	40%	82%	32.8	36
Total			85.3	90

TABLE 8.2   Cycle Time: Responding to Customer Inquiries for Product Information

MAIL		PHONE	
Average Performance	Score	Average Performance	Score
Less than 24 hours	100	Less than 1 hour	100
24–27 hours	95	1–2 hours	95
27–32 hours	90	2–3 hours	90
32–36 hours	85	3–4 hours	85

convert raw data into summary scores, you need to develop scales for assigning scores to performance levels. An example is shown in Table 8.2 for a customer service department where the cycle time for responding to customer inquiries is tracked and summarized. Cycle time is tracked for situations where customers call in for catalogs or product literature (mail). Cycle time for this measure is the elapsed time between when the customer call is received and when the package is sent to the customer (all packages sent by 2-day Priority Mail). Responding to customer requests with a callback on the telephone is also tracked. Calls where customer questions/inquiries can be handled on the same call are not included in these data. An alternative to a scale in Table 8.2 might be to perform a calculation on the cycle time data to arrive at an actual percentage score out of a possible 100.

MEASURING EMPLOYEE SAFETY

For virtually all manufacturing and many other types of organizations, measurement of employee safety is of paramount importance. Most organizations do actually measure safety and many include safety as one of the key metrics in their overall scorecard that is reviewed by executives. The problems with most measures of safety are that they focus on the past and they relate to the incidence of safety problems. Typical safety measures include the following:

- Lost-time accidents.
- Accident severity ratings.
- Worker compensation costs.
- OSHA audits.

A good overall safety index should be part of many organization's scorecard if employee safety is an issue. A bank or financial services firm might be allowed to do without a safety index. Getting a paper cut or being strangled by a telephone cord might not warrant a safety index. In putting together a safety index, it should be similar to a customer satisfaction index, which we discussed in Chapter 6, or an overall process index, which we discussed in this chapter. A safety index should consist of several output measures like lost-time accidents or worker compensation costs, along with several preventive measures such as near misses, or safety audits designed to document unsafe behaviors or conditions that could lead to accidents. The key is to have several preventive measures in your index that allow you to identify conditions that may lead to safety problems. Pacific Bell and Air Products and Chemicals both have very good approaches for measuring and controlling safety. Both organizations have developed safety metrics that focus on safe employee behavior (the process) rather than simply on the output measures such as accidents.

ENVIRONMENTAL AND COMMUNITY METRICS

Most of this book has focused on designing a measurement system that considers the needs of stockholders, customers, and employees. However, all organizations also have stakeholders whose needs need to be identified. Measures of how well an organization satisfies its stakeholders may also need to be included in the scorecard. For many organizations, environmental measures are important enough to include in the macro scorecard that executives monitor on a regular basis. An oil or chemical company would certainly be expected to have good measures of its environmental performance on emissions or wastewater purity. Because executives probably don't want to see 22 different graphs relating to environmental performance, it may be helpful to develop an index of overall performance in this area. The index should be comprised of preventive or process metrics as well as output metrics, just like the safety index previously discussed.

Organizations have many stakeholders besides the communities in which they have facilities. One organization tracks the number of hours its employees spend each month working for volunteer, charity, or community groups. The company prides itself on being a good corporate citizen, and employees are expected to spend a minimum of 12 hours per month on community service. The company pays its employees for 8 hours a month for that community service as well, and gives them a day off to do it. Another organization considers ethics to be very important; it tracks the ethics level of the company once a month by counting the number of calls it receives to its ethics "hot line" and assigning a severity rating to each call, depending on the violation. You may want to consider adding one or two metrics to your other process metrics that deal with safety, environmental, and community involvement performance. Safety might fit better under the employee box in your scorecard, or you could decide to put it here. Which category or box you place the metric under is not really important—just don't forget it altogether.

FUTURE-ORIENTED PROCESS METRICS

I mention earlier the problem of having all of your metrics focus on measuring the past. Organizations that want to achieve a future vision must measure how well they are progressing along the path toward their vision. These future-oriented process metrics are important, but very difficult to identify and measure objectively. Owens Corning, the Toledo-based building materials manufacturer embarked on a new approach to selling in the 1980s. Rather than having their salespeople concentrate on selling to contractors and builders, they felt it would be more effective to sell their products to architects and designers at the conceptual design stage. By getting them to specify Owens Corning products in building designs up front, the contractor would not need to be sold. Makes sense, right? The problem came in measuring this performance. Architects might initially specify Owens Corning insulation or one of their other products in the initial design and then change their mind as the design or budget changed before actual construction began. Paying salespeople a commission based on getting products into the design turned out to be a mistake, because designs are revised many times before they are finalized and are often still changing as the structure or building is being constructed. The company finally developed an effective metric in which salespeople received points based on the dollar value of the product that was specified, and the stage in the design process at which Owens Corning products were included in the specifications.

Rockwater, an undersea oil rig construction firm mentioned by Kaplan and Norton in their videotape on the balanced scorecard, tried to come up with a similar future-oriented process metric. Rockwater wanted to get potential customers to consider their firm's strengths in the conceptual design phase of a construction project so the project would go to Rockwater without having to go out for competitive bids. The metric they picked for their scorecard was the number of hours spent discussing potential new work with customers. This sounds like a logical metric, but another company found that this metric was impossible to track objectively. Data had to be self-reported by salespeople and engineers, and they knew the company considered it important. They often "fudged" the figures, indicating that they has spent six hours a week discussing new work with customers, when in fact they were often discussing sports, current events, or an existing project.

In spite of the difficulty in doing so, it is important to track process metrics that will help promote the future success of the organization. Any metric that is based on a subjective evaluation of human behavior can lead to problems. You don't want a measurement system that promotes busy employees engaging in nonvalue-added behavior. You also don't want to solely focus on measuring outputs, because these are historical types of metrics. The key to effective future-oriented process metrics is to conduct research to ensure that the process metrics lead to important outputs. Don't just do a logic test. Most process metrics that drive the wrong performance end up passing the logic test. A second rule for ensuring that you have selected the right future-oriented process metrics is to select those that can be measured reliably and consistently. Owens Corning could verify the specification of their products in building designs, and did not have to rely on the word of their salespeople. You often don't need to put money on a metric to encourage cheating, but if you do, you could really have a problem.

HOW EXCELLENT ORGANIZATIONS MEASURE PROCESSES AND OPERATIONAL RESULTS

- Cycle time for all key processes is measured.

- Rework time and/or costs are tracked for key production and service delivery processes.

- Key measures of productivity are identified and tracked for major processes in the organization.

- Key processes have been identified in each unit, function, and department of the organization, and process measures have been defined for each key process.

- Process measures are correlated directly with product/service characteristics or performance factors that are of prime importance to customers.

- Standards or goals are set for all key process measures, and those standards are based upon benchmark organizations and customer requirements.

- Process measures promote a preventive approach to achieving consistently high-quality products and services.

- The organization has developed an overall safety index that is tracked at least once a month, and consists of several output measures like lost-time accidents, as well as a number of preventive or behavioral measures.

- A few future-oriented process measures are tracked that will help ensure long-term survival and success.

Measuring Supplier Performance

Many organizations spend more money buying goods and services from suppliers than they spend running their own parts of the business. A chemical company I worked with spends 66 cents out of every dollar on suppliers. A company in the beef or pork business spends about 80 to 90 cents of every dollar it spends buying pigs or cows. Suppliers are critical to most organizations, and many organizations do a very poor job of measuring supplier performance. In this chapter, we'll talk about some of the mistakes companies make when tracking supplier performance and provide you with some guidelines to do a better job of tracking how your suppliers perform.

VALUES AND BELIEFS REGARDING SUPPLIERS

An organization's values and beliefs regarding suppliers impact how suppliers are treated and how their performance is monitored. Currently, most organizations talk about how they partner with their suppliers and work with them in a cooperative fashion. This is, however, nothing but rhetoric in many industries. Some larger organizations realize that they have the upper hand with suppliers, and often exploit that advantage unfairly. Following the lead of Delta, the other major airlines recently decided that they would cut travel agents' commissions from the previous 10 percent of the ticket price to a flat $50 per ticket. The agents' commissions were a major cost to the airlines, and reducing these fees increased their profitability. The result is that the airlines have alienated their most important suppliers and caused many to go out of business. In retaliation for this drastic drop in commissions, travel agents now charge customers a fee for services that were previously free. Now, in addition to the price

of the airline ticket, a $10 handling fee is charged every time the agent is-
sues a ticket, and an additional fee for changes to itinerary. The travel
agent has also started charging for other services that were previously
free, such as hotel and car reservations. In effect, the airlines have raised
their prices to the consumers, which has angered both the travel agents
and the airlines' customers.

Other examples can be found in many industries where the big companies use their power to control suppliers. In the early 1980s, a large
automotive company sent out a letter to all suppliers suggesting they
"voluntarily" cut invoices by 10 percent for six months because this automotive company was having a bad year. The suppliers met to decide
what to do. Because 10 percent was about all the profit there was on any
material or service, the only recourse was to raise prices to this automotive company by 10 percent and then voluntarily comply with its wish to
cut 10 percent from the invoices. Some were unable to raise prices because of locked-in contracts, but found ways of making up the 10 percent by cutting corners on quality and in other areas. A few others simply refused to do business with the company if they had to cut their
prices. The bottom line is that the strategy did not work very well—just
like the airlines' strategy does not seem to be working very well with the
travel agents.

Most organizations have a set of unwritten rules and beliefs that govern employee behavior with suppliers. These rules and beliefs have a
great impact on how supplier performance is measured. The government
procurement system, for example, is based upon the belief that suppliers
cannot be trusted and will take advantage of you at every opportunity.
The system is also based on a lack of trust of their own employees. Strict
rules and regulations are enforced and suppliers are not even allowed to
buy a cup of coffee for government customers.

When I worked in Detroit in the late 1970s and early 1980s, some
managers in the Big 3 automotive companies all operated under the belief
system that suppliers should be exploited for personal gain as much as
possible. We had to buy vacations for automotive executives, and expensive gifts like televisions or sets of golf clubs, and hire their kids every
summer when they came home from college. These were just expected,
and the clients had no qualms asking for them. Changing your belief system related to how suppliers should be treated is an essential first step in
building cooperative relationships with them.

HOW MANY ORGANIZATIONS MEASURE SUPPLIER PERFORMANCE

Most small companies still don't really measure supplier performance. They check the materials they buy when delivered, and if an item is not right, send it back. Tracking supplier performance and charting it are thought to be more trouble than they are worth. Small companies cannot afford an army of inspectors and technicians who collect samples and evaluate them based on predetermined standards. Large companies or organizations have reams of data on suppliers, but most of these are not the right type of data. Most large companies inspect incoming shipments from suppliers and collect detailed data on the extent that supplier products meet their standards. These data are fed back to suppliers and used to evaluate their performance. Large organizations also typically collect data on the percentage of supplier shipments that arrive on time to their loading dock. Rather than have a supplier report card that includes 50 different quality measures with scores on each, you need to select the vital few key measures (6 to 10). Another good way of simplifying the product/service quality section of your supplier report card is to score the suppliers' performance on each individual product/service quality measure and assign a weight to each one, depending upon its importance to you. This way you can compute an overall product/service quality index for each supplier. An example is shown in Table 9.1 for suppliers who repair your computer systems.

The example shown in the table is simple because it includes only three measures, but you might have many more on your report card, which makes it more important to summarize the data into an overall index. The data on supplier product/service quality should be based on your inspections, not the suppliers', so you might want to list the batch/box

TABLE 9.1   Product/Service Quality Dimensions

Product/Service Quality Dimensions	Score	Weight	Weighted Score
Percent problems fixed right the first time	80%	50%	40
Timeliness of arrival	68%	25%	17
Timeliness of job completion	75%	25%	18.75
Total score			75.75/100

from which you took the sample, so if there are problems, suppliers can trace them back to their root cause.

MEASURING CUSTOMER SATISFACTION

This is the section of the supplier's report card where you get to rate them, based on your opinions of how well they performed for you. At the simplest level, you could simply assign a supplier an overall rating on a 1-to-10 scale, based on how it performed. This is easy on your part, but it may not help the supplier much. A better approach is to break down customer satisfaction into your most important requirements and grade how the supplier performed in each area. A summary score or index can then be prepared, just as you did for the product/service quality performance data. Some dimensions for which you might evaluate supplier performance in this area include the following:

- Responsiveness.
- Flexibility.
- Attention to detail.
- Ease of doing business.
- Courteousness of staff.
- Follow-through.

The dimensions with which you evaluate your satisfaction levels with suppliers should be based on what is important to you as the buyer. In defining these requirements, it may be helpful to talk to different people in your organization. Individuals who buy supplier goods and services may have a different set of needs from individuals who use the supplier goods or services. Both views are important. The customer satisfaction factors do not need to be tailored to different types of suppliers. They can be generic and should apply to all the suppliers. One dimension of your satisfaction that I recommend keeping as a separate part of the supplier report card is price and/or value.

MEASURING PRICE/VALUE

The only kind of service for which price is not important is one that is free. I get great service from Sundance Travel, my biggest supplier. I spend about $75,000 a year on airplane tickets, hotels, and rental cars, so I am very particular about accuracy and attention to detail, and Sundance, my travel agent, almost always pays attention to the details and gets them right. Price or value was not an issue until recently, because I never had to pay for the service. All travel agency services were free to me, so all I cared about was quality. Not anymore. As I mentioned earlier in this chapter, Sundance, along with other travel agencies, has started charging for services that used to be free. All of a sudden, value and price have become an issue. Some agencies charge lower fees than mine, so there is a possibility that I may start hunting for a new supplier, even though I'm delighted with Sundance's service.

Price or perceived value is almost always one of the most important dimensions to measure when evaluating supplier performance. I recently flew from Los Angeles to London on United's Connoisseur (business) class. Service was great, and the plane even took off and landed on time. However, the ticket cost almost $5,000! People sitting in coach probably paid $600 for their ticket, and there was a man next to me who bought a coach ticket for around $1,100 and used his international upgrades to move up to business class. If United had asked me how I perceived the value I got for my $5,000 ticket, I would say that I felt ripped off. Sure, service was good, but $5,000 is a ridiculous amount of money to spend for an airplane ticket anywhere.

Price is less important when it's the company's or client's money that is being spent, rather than your own, but it is still important. Most of us are always looking for ways to avoid our employers getting ripped off by suppliers. When evaluating your suppliers' performance, it is important to give them separate feedback on their prices or fees relative to their competitors, along with your perceptions about their prices and the value you received for your money. You might have a 5-point scale that ranges from 1 = "I feel totally ripped off" to 5 = "You don't charge nearly enough for your product/service," but I doubt that anyone would give you a 5 rating.

What I recommend is one hard measure of price, where you indicate the extent to which the price of the suppliers' product or service deviates from that of major competitors. You also need a soft measure in the supplier report card, where you rate them on the value of their product/service for the price. Restaurants and hotels often ask this on their survey cards, because perceived value has so much impact on customer satisfaction levels. The Ritz-Carlton Hotel in Pasadena is one of the nicest hotels in Los Angeles. The service and the accommodations are both great, as one might expect. But, the best part of the deal is that the rooms are only $160 a night, which I thought was a real bargain for the Ritz. So, I perceived that I got a lot for my money from the Ritz-Carlton.

MEASURING KEY PROCESS VARIABLES

Up to this point, we have been discussing measures of suppliers' past performance. We inspect their products, rate their service, and make a judgment on the value of our purchases. A key part of any supplier report card consists of process or preventive measures that help the customer and supplier anticipate potential problems down the road. Cargill, the large agricultural organization, is a major supplier of corn syrup to Coca-Cola. Rather than inspect the syrup at its own processing plants, Coca-Cola requires Cargill to provide key process data on a daily basis. Both companies have eliminated unnecessary paperwork and delays by having Cargill monitor process variables in the manufacturing of the corn syrup, report these data to Coke, and ship the syrup directly to Coca-Cola's production lines. Inspection is not necessary because Cargill has proven that it can maintain Coke's strict quality standards by controlling process variables. In some businesses, it makes a great deal of sense to eliminate product or output inspections by simply monitoring process variables. However, this only makes sense when the processes and process variables can be controlled with a great deal of precision. Asking for process measures from suppliers also only makes sense when there is solid research that shows a direct link between process variables and output quality and consistency.

With processes that depend a great deal on human behavior, or where the process is not 90 percent science, process measures may be inappropriate. For example, let's suppose that one of your most important type of suppliers are your dealers or distributors who sell your products to customers. Following the logic of process measurement and control, you would not need to look at the sales (outputs) figures from your distributors. Instead, you would ask them for data on various measures of the selling and distribution processes. Processes measures for the selling process might include the following:

- Number of leads/contacts made with potential new customers.
- Number of requests for quotations written.

- Amount of time spent discussing needs with existing customers.
- Number of relationship-building activities with existing customers.

The problem with measuring process variables for a process that is far from being a hard science, like selling, is that the process measures might look great, but the output measures could still look terrible. Selling is certainly not a science like manufacturing aluminum or corn syrup. Hence, process measures are not very important from the customer's standpoint. I would recommend asking suppliers for process data in situations where the process measures are directly linked with your requirements for the suppliers' products or services.

MEASURING SUPPLIERS ON HOW THEY RUN THEIR ORGANIZATIONS

Many large organizations have drastically reduced the number of suppliers from which they regularly buy products and services. Some large companies like Xerox have reduced their number of suppliers by more than 50 percent. This sorting process has narrowed down suppliers to not only ones that provide good products/services at a fair price, but suppliers that manage their businesses effectively. Large organizations are very dependent upon their suppliers, so they want to make sure that if they partner with a supplier, the supplier company is well-managed, so that they will be around for the long haul. Just as organizations tend to hire people that fit into their culture, they pick their suppliers the same way. Companies that are teamwork-oriented tend to work with suppliers that are teamwork-oriented, for example.

ISO 9000

A number of large organizations today do much more than provide suppliers with periodic report cards on their performance; they audit suppliers on how they run their organizations. This was relatively unheard of 10 years ago, but has become quite common among large organizations. A number of large organizations around the world require that their suppliers be ISO-9000-certified. The ISO certification process looks at basic production and distribution processes and documentation, and focuses on systems for minimizing variability in a company's work processes. The beauty of ISO 9000 is that it provides a common set of standards or criteria that suppliers must adhere to each year to maintain their certification. Buying from an ISO-certified supplier helps ensure that the company is buying from a supplier that has the basics of a good-quality system in place. Using ISO certification as a standard criterion for supplier selection has saved millions of dollars by eliminating the need for each company to have its own supplier certification process. The automotive industry in the United States has created its own version of the ISO criteria that it will be requiring all suppliers to meet in the next couple of years. The criteria are very close to the ISO, but include a number of specific items that are peculiar to the automotive industry. Automotive folks I talk to think that the automotive industry standards are more difficult to meet than the generic ISO criteria.

Supplier Baldrige Audits

Another type of periodic supplier assessment that is becoming more and more popular is an evaluation against the Malcolm Baldrige Award criteria. Motorola actually requires its suppliers to write an application and apply for the award so they can receive feedback. Motorola believes that the application process and feedback received from examiners can go a long way to help a company improve. Although this is certainly true, a number of suppliers did not take Motorola's suggestion very seriously; they put in a minimum amount of effort to apply for the award just to get Motorola off their backs.

Other organizations do not require actual application for the award, but use the award criteria to evaluate supplier organizations. One of the companies that pioneered this effort is Pacific Bell. It asks suppliers to complete a written application for its own supplier awards program, uses trained Pacific Bell examiners to assess supplier applications, and awards different levels of certification to suppliers based on their scores. Using the gold, silver, and bronze award scheme of the Olympics, Pacific Bell certifies key suppliers based on their scores on the applications. Becoming a "Gold"-level Pac Bell supplier results in not only a nice trophy and recognition, it helps cement the supplier's partnership with Pac Bell for the long term. Joe Yacura, the Pacific Bell vice president who designed this certification program, has recently taken the job of vice president of American Express's international procurement function, and has implemented a very similar program at American Express. Some of the key measures relating to supplier performance that American Express now tracks are as follows:

- Scores on assessment against the Baldrige criteria.

- Percentage of key suppliers participating in the certification program each year.

- Number of gold, silver, and bronze suppliers each year.

LINKING SUPPLIER PERFORMANCE MEASURES TO KEY BUSINESS DRIVERS

Organizations make the same mistakes when measuring supplier performance that they do when measuring other areas of performance. They tend to measure things that are easy to count and report on, and fail to link the measures to their key success factors. One way of making sure that suppliers are measured on the most importance variables is to develop different report cards for different classifications of suppliers. This has been done by a number of organizations, and it becomes too complex and labor-intensive to gather, report, and interpret the data. Having a generic set of measurement categories is preferred.

One simple way of linking supplier measures to key success factors is to assign a weight to the four generic supplier performance measurement discussed earlier, based on the relative importance of each. For a components supplier, perhaps the highly weighted measures are product quality and just-in-time delivery. For a service supplier like one that repairs your office equipment and computers, the key measures might be the cost of equipment downtime and repeat calls for the same problem. For the company that sells paper, the highest weighted measure might be competitive pricing. Assigning importance weights to supplier measures allows you the flexibility of having a generic supplier report card format that focuses on the four areas of (1) product/service quality, (2) customer satisfaction, (3) price/value, and (4) process performance. Importance weights can be applied to each of the four categories and to the specific measures within each category. This approach allows you the flexibility of tailoring each report card to each supplier and linking what's important for its performance to your key business drivers. An example is shown in Table 9.2 of a company that provides public relations services for a management consulting firm.

Based on this example, the consulting firm is really concerned with the amount and types of exposure that PR firms are able to generate, because this can be directly linked to business opportunities. Process mea-

TABLE 9.2   Example of Supplier Performance Measures and Weights for a Public Relations Firm

Product/Service Quality		**50%**
Consulting leads derived from exposure	20%	
Frequency of name in media	10%	
Amount of coverage	5%	
Quality/accuracy of coverage	5%	
Targeted publications/programs	10%	
Customer Satisfaction		**25%**
Minimize our time/hassle	10%	
Responsiveness to our needs	4%	
Understanding of our business	6%	
Timeliness of work	5%	
Price/Value		**15%**
Price versus other competitive firms	5%	
Our perceptions of value vs. cost per month	10%	
Process Measures		**10%**
Actual billings vs. budget	4%	
Activity to generate exposure	3%	
Thorough documentation of activity	3%	

sures are given a very low weight in this report card, because doing good public relations work is hardly an exact science. You can have a PR firm that bills you lots of hours for lots of activity that leads to very limited exposure. The consulting firm is not very interested in the processes the firm follows to get them exposure in the media. It is concerned with the accomplishments of the PR firm and that doing business with them is as hassle-free as possible.

WHICH SUPPLIERS TO MEASURE

Although I'm a supplier to some large and sophisticated organizations, I've never received a supplier report card or any formal feedback/assessment from any of them, even though I'm providing important training and consulting services to these organizations. In the overall scheme of things, Mark Graham Brown & Associates is a fairly small supplier to all of these organizations. My biggest clients might hire me for 50 days a year, which is a major investment to me, but a drop in the bucket in the expenses of a company such as IBM. When measuring supplier performance and formally tracking it, it makes sense to follow the 80/20 rule, or Pareto principle. Most organizations spend 80 percent of their expenses with 20 percent of their suppliers. These are the ones whose performance should be tracked with your report card system. The other minor suppliers will get feedback in less formal ways such as repeat orders or loss of your account. It is important that you do not go overboard in designing a measurement system that is too complex and difficult to administer.

HOW EXCELLENT COMPANIES MEASURE SUPPLIER PERFORMANCE

- The company collects data on key product/service variables for the goods and services it buys from suppliers.

- Dimensions of supplier quality that are measured are linked to the company's key success factors.

- Measures of satisfaction with supplier performance are collected on a regular basis.

- Suppliers regularly give feedback to the companies that purchase their products/services.

- Suppliers are rated on their pricing and how it compares to their chief competitors.

- Suppliers are assessed using key process metrics along with the traditional quality and price metrics.

- Major suppliers are audited using a set of criteria such as ISO 9000 or the Baldrige Award criteria.

Measuring Employee Satisfaction

Take away my people, but leave my factories, and soon grass will grow on the factory floors. Take away my factories, but leave my people, and soon we will have a new and better factory.

—Andrew Carnegie

Currently, most employees feel lucky to have a job, are not expecting lifetime employment, or that their employers will care about their growth and self-actualization as individuals. Having a reasonably well-paying job that makes use of our skills and does not require 80 hours a week of work is a rare commodity these days. Employers realize that they have the upper hand and do even less than they did in the past to look after the well-being of employees. It's a buyer's market out there. If you're not happy with your job or organization, there's a hoard of well-educated Generation-Xers out there who would be glad to have your job for a much smaller salary than you're receiving.

THE EMPLOYEE COMES FIRST, NOT THE CUSTOMER

This concept is a radical philosophy in today's world of downsizing or rightsizing, or whatever other euphemism we use for laying off employees. Some organizations have found that satisfying or delighting employees is a prerequisite to satisfying or delighting customers. Unhappy employees who are motivated by fear of losing their jobs are never going to give 120 percent of their effort for very long. Fear is a powerful motivator, but it's a temporary one. As soon as the threat is lifted, or someone stops watching, performance declines.

A few of the more forward-thinking companies really believe that delighting their employees is a sound business strategy as well as being a humanistic approach to running a business. One company that puts this philosophy to better use than most is Baldrige Award winner AT&T Universal Card Systems. Formed as a business in 1990, this credit card company used the Baldrige Award criteria as the framework for building its company. It built a company of winners by handpicking individuals from the best credit card companies up and down the East Coast and convincing them to come to Jacksonville to work for AT&T's new credit card company. Aside from the low cost of living in Northern Florida, AT&T pays these individuals quite a bit more than the other credit card companies pay for similar jobs. It also allows employees to earn cash bonuses based on their own and company performance. Child care assistance, an on-site health club, the best and safest equipment, and a wide variety of additional employee services help ensure that AT&T UCS's employees believe that they work for one of the best companies in America.

The approach has paid off well beyond delighted employees. The company has made a mark as one of the biggest and most successful credit card companies in an industry where there are over 6,000 competitors. In fact, in their first 20 months in business, AT&T UCS ranked third in the industry in the total number of customers. All this was accomplished without an ad campaign and with interest rates that were about average. Customers were won through word-of-mouth referrals and through direct mail solicitation. I spent two days in Jacksonville at the company and was so impressed, I traded in my bank card for an AT&T card as soon as I got home. Part of the company's success strategy is to be as selective about choosing customers as it is in choosing employees. It only wants the best.

HOW MOST ORGANIZATIONS ADDRESS EMPLOYEE SATISFACTION

Most organizations just really don't care about employee satisfaction. Sure, they all have a mission or vision statement in the lobby that proclaims something like; "Employees are our greatest asset." The problem with these value or mission statements is that that is all they are—words on the wall. Most organizations operate as if employees are one of their least important assets. For example, a major Fortune 500 corporation recently had its Human Resources (HR) Vice President retire. The corporation chose not to replace him, but to add the HR responsibilities to another vice president's job, who already had a number of other support functions to look after and had no experience with HR. This action sent a powerful message to employees. The whole HR function is not really very important. The corporation wouldn't even consider not having a Vice President of Finance, of Engineering, or of most of the other important functions. This organization, like many, measures employee satisfaction with an employee morale survey that is conducted every 2 to 3 years. Many companies have stopped doing morale surveys because they sets up an expectation that it needs to do something about employee morale problems. The sentiment of most employees regarding surveys is as follows:

> Yeah, they did an employee survey here a couple of years ago. They gave us an edited version of the results in the newsletter and then we never heard anything more. We kind of thought some things might change as a result of the survey, but nothing did.

Most organizations also conduct exit interviews as a way of gathering employee satisfaction data. The HR representative dutifully records notes in the employee's personnel file, files it away, and nothing happens with the data. Turnover data are also collected by most medium and large organizations. If turnover data are collected, it's almost never reviewed by executives, unless there is a major problem with employees leaving in droves.

IMPROVING PROFITS THROUGH DOWNSIZING

Improving profits by downsizing has become the preferred strategy of the 1990s for all types of organizations. Wall Street tends to reward these downsizing efforts because they almost always improve short-term profits. IBM has cut about half of its workforce over the last couple of years, as have a number of other large corporations. The balance sheet looks better temporarily, but the true impact of the loss of all these knowledgeable employees will be felt years from now. One of the short-term detrimental effects of downsizing is that stress levels are at an all-time high in most large organizations. Many in middle and upper management are routinely putting in 70 to 80 hours a week, with no signs of the workload decreasing.

STUDIES CASTS DOUBT ON THE VALUE OF DOWNSIZING

If everyone's doing it, downsizing must work, right? Not necessarily. Downsizing is like dieting. It works to produce short-term results, but almost always fails to produce sustained weight loss. Downsizing makes an organization look good on the bottom line for a year, but the long-term benefits are questionable. Arthur D. Little, Inc., one of the most respected management consulting firms in the world, recently completed a study on the impact of downsizing. A summary of the study appeared in the September/October 1994 edition of the Quality Productivity and Management Association's (QPMA) *Discovery*. Of the 350 executives who responded to the survey, 70 percent said that they had more problems than they expected with their downsizing efforts. Less than 16 percent said they had achieved the goals they set for their downsizing efforts, and 40 percent said that they were displeased with all of their results from downsizing.

Another study conducted by the Census Bureau's Center for Economic Study suggests that increases in productivity are not necessarily due to downsizing efforts. The study looked at 140,000 factories during the 1980s. Almost half (45 percent) of the factories that showed gains in productivity had growing workforces.

HOW MANY COMPANIES TREAT THEIR EMPLOYEES

Your competitors can copy your products and services in just about any industry. As soon as you come up with something unique and different, your competition has a similar product or service on the market that is often less expensive, or perhaps has more features than yours. One hotel starts turning down guests beds at night and leaving a little chocolate on the pillow, and 3 months later, they're all doing it. IBM comes out with a new laptop computer that has more features and power than anything else on the market in that price range, and a knock-off version is in the stores a few months later. It's difficult to differentiate your company anymore, no matter what business you are in. Leading organizations have found that the only thing their competitors cannot steal is their people. But that's not really true either. Companies raid their competitors quite often, stealing their best people.

If you've invested a lot of money to attract the best and most talented people to your organization, and spent a fortune training them, the last thing you want to do is lose them to the competition. So, how do you keep your good people? How do you prevent your best employees from walking when a headhunter calls with an offer of $10,000 more a year than you are paying someone? Paying the highest salaries in the industry is not the answer either. I did some consulting work with one of the major oil companies that was having a problem with turnover among its scientists and engineers. Many of what it thought were its "superstar" technical people were leaving the company after 5 to 8 years. This was the period when they were really becoming the most valuable to the company. This particular oil company was known to have one of the best compensation and benefits packages in the industry. All the engineers and scientists I interviewed felt that they were well paid. In fact, some of them confidentially told me that they felt like they were overpaid for the work they were doing. An analysis of exit interview data revealed that many were leaving for the same or even less money. They were quitting because the work they did was mundane and way beneath their technical abilities. These people were turned on by a challenge, the chance to exercise their intellectual and management skills.

Upper management refused to deal with the issue once it was brought to its attention as to the reason it was losing some of their best technical people. The feeling was that these young people had unrealistic expectations and had to pay their dues, performing mundane tasks for 5 to 10 years just as upper management had done. So, the company continued to recruit the smartest people from the best schools, luring them with high salaries and the promise of challenging and interesting work. And these same people continued to leave the company for the same reasons as their predecessors about the time that the company was getting its return on investment in training them. These kind of figures never show up on the balance sheet, and the turnover is easy to rationalize.

The Big 6 accounting and consulting firms have a similar approach to the management of their human resources. As a Baldrige Examiner, I evaluated one of these large accounting firms; it lost a lot of points because of its whole approach to managing its human resources and to ensuring that these people do good-quality work. This firm was like its competitors in that it went out to a few select universities every year and recruited the best and the brightest. Getting a job right out of school with one of these large firms is quite an accomplishment. The firm hires 250 new recruits every year, spends several months training them, and closely supervises their work for 3 or more years, until they are fairly good auditors, financial advisors, or consultants.

After 3 years of working 80 hours a week, having to redo their work often seven or eight times, most of those 250 new recruits are gone. Those who are really sharp are hired away by a client and end up only working 40 hours a week. Many others become frustrated with the whole profession, realizing that it will take 10 or 20 years of 80-hour weeks to ever make partner and get the big bucks. Some are asked to leave because their work is not up to par or they are simply unwilling to completely give up their personal lives. So, after 3 or 4 years, the firm is left with about 25 of the original 250 recruits. Are they the cream of the crop out of the 250? Probably not. This firm, like many, wasted hundreds of thousands of dollars every year in recruiting and training many new employees, and did nothing to try to recoup its investment. A more preventive approach that would have resulted in a better score from Baldrige is to hire 50 new employees, spend the time training and coaching them, and have them stay at least five years so the company could get back its investment in them. This approach would require a lot more careful screening up front and perhaps being more honest with the new recruits about what life will be like working for the firm.

HOW EMPLOYEE SATISFACTION LINKS TO SERVICE AND PROFITS

Any executive will tell you that employee satisfaction or morale is important to organizational success. The problem comes when it is time to spend money on efforts to improve employee satisfaction. Many executives are just not convinced that high morale necessarily leads to better quality or improved financial performance. In fact, sometimes it does not. My first job out of college was with a training and consulting firm in Detroit that really believed in the importance of delighting employees. We didn't have any values posted on the wall, but everyone understood that the most important things were first to delight the clients and then have fun at our jobs. We always went overboard to delight our clients; most of the time we did have fun at work. The company consisted of about 200 mostly young and talented people who worked and partied hard.

The company president was largely responsible for the culture in this organization. His personal priorities were also to go beyond what we had promised to our clients, and to have fun while we were doing it. In our efforts to delight our customers and employees, we often went over budget on projects, and never really did well on our financial results. I remember that back in the early 1980s, our goal was to get 2 percent profits, and we never reached that goal. I still miss working at this company. It was like an extension of college, and we all had a great deal of fun while working on client projects. What this company failed to do, however, is to balance delighting customers and employees with making money. I went back to visit my old friends at this company about five years ago and was shocked to see how much it had changed. It had been acquired by a large firm that was very concerned with profits, and the whole place had a different feel. Yes, it was now profitable, but the whole place had this quiet, serious air, so that I could just tell it was not the fun place it used to be.

I think that you don't need to trade off one thing for another, however. It is possible to make money, and delight your customers and employees all at the same time. I've seen enough companies that do it to make me a believer. In fact, I think that focusing on delighting employees is directly related to your customer satisfaction levels and financial success. In a recent article, J. L. Hesket et al. ("Putting the Service-Profit Chain to Work," *Harvard Business Review,* March/April 1994) make a strong case for the link between employee satisfaction and productivity, employee retention, product/service quality, and customer satisfaction. The authors use Southwest Airlines as an example. Here we have a company that has high levels of employee and customer satisfaction, and is one of the most profitable airlines, due to employee productivity levels. Southwest has about 40 percent higher employee and aircraft utilization than their competitors. Southwest Airlines was recently named as one of the country's 10 best places to work due to its efforts to delight employees. The key to achieving high levels of customer and employee satisfaction, along with excellent financial results, is balance. Companies such as Southwest and Home Depot teach managers how to make all areas of performance a priority, without sacrificing one for the others.

INTELLECTUAL CAPITAL

As more organizations become more knowledge-based, the knowledge and skills of employees will increasingly become an important asset or liability. Research-and-development firms, software companies, and others already realize that the intellectual power of their workforce is one of the most valuable assets that needs to be protected and nurtured. Pacific Bell is one such company that does a good job tracking the competencies of its employees and using a variety of data to measure employee satisfaction. For these sorts of things to happen, upper management has to believe that employee competencies are truly an asset that can be measured and something that is as important and valuable as money in the bank. These enlightened organizations often believe that intellectual capital is even more valuable than money. Employees may come up with ideas that earn you millions of dollars, and even the most talented employees usually don't cost that much.

One of the measures that is included in the employee portion of Air Products and Chemicals' corporate scorecard is the number of hours of training received by each employee. Technology gives this company an advantage over its competitors. Like many of the world's best companies that focus on employee development, Air Products strives to provide each employee with an average of 80 hours of training per year. That's two complete weeks of training every single year. Most employees in most organizations receive a couple of days training a year. Air Products makes a measure of employee training part of its overall scorecard because it wants to make sure that training is emphasized, and that it actually occurs. Measuring business unit executives on how much training they give their people as part of their overall evaluation helps ensure that training budgets are not cut to help improve profits.

Hours of training per year is actually a rather gross measure, sometimes encouraging lots of poor-quality training where people never really learn anything, but the amount of training an organization provides for employees is a fairly good indicator of its commitment to continually developing its workforce. Eventually, Air Products plans to implement more refined measures that are based on the effectiveness of the training, rather than just the amount of it. Three-time Baldrige winner AT&T is an organization that superbly tracks the effectiveness of its employee development and training in many of its larger business units. New England Telephone is another organization that collects some good measures on the effectiveness of training.

Many organizations measure the amount and effectiveness of the training they do. What is unique about some of the organizations I've mentioned is that the CEO and all the vice presidents look at training statistics on a regular basis, as a way of evaluating the progress of the entire company. Executives in these enlightened companies realize that human capital is important to measure as a way of ensuring the company's long-term survival and success.

DETERMINING EMPLOYEE REQUIREMENTS

In Chapter 6, I emphasized the need to segment customers and spend a lot of time up front digging to find out what their hot buttons are. Very few organizations do a thorough job of this with their customers, and almost no companies that I'm aware of do this with their employees. Most just assume that employees all want the same things: security, a good paycheck, interesting work, and a nice work environment. Although this may be true, doing the basics may just be enough to satisfy employees. A satisfied employee is like a satisfied customer. He or she will walk as soon as someone comes along with a slightly better offer. A delighted employee will not only never leave, but will tell the world about what a great company he or she works for. If you are serious about delighting your employees, and think that delighted employees are much more likely to put out 120 percent effort every day, you'll need to spend some time and money to find out what it takes to delight them.

The first thing to do is to segment employees based upon common needs. This will take some thought before you automatically sort employees according to gender, seniority, or job grade level. Employees' personal situations and goals have a lot to do with what is needed to delight them. For example, a single mother with three small children may have very different priorities from a 50-year-old married mom whose children are all grown and out of the house. Keep in mind that no matter what you do, you will never satisfy everybody all the time. Just like dealing with customers, you want to try to delight most of your employees most of the time.

The methods used to determine employee needs, requirements, and priorities are the same as those used to determine customer requirements: focus groups, interviews, surveys, satisfaction feedback, and exit interviews are all good sources of data. Whatever method you use, the key to having a good approach is to ask the right questions and to use multiple data-gathering methods. Another key is not to do it once every three years. Employee priorities change just as customers' do and need to be assessed on a regular basis.

EMPLOYEE SATISFACTION SURVEYS

If you do nothing else, at least do an annual employee morale or climate survey. I would recommend using an outside firm that specializes in these surveys for several reasons. First of all, the cost will probably end up to be about the same as doing it in-house. Employee surveys usually cost around $5 to $10 per survey to send out and have the results reported. So, if you survey a random sample of 1,000 employees, the survey will cost you $5,000 to $10,000. This is probably less than you spend in a week to gather and report financial data. Another reason to use an outside firm is that you can see how your employee satisfaction levels compare to other companies. Large survey firms should have a database with which you can compare your own results to see how far you are from others in your industry, or from benchmark-level companies. A disadvantage of using an outside survey firm is that you may not be allowed to customize the survey with questions tailored to the needs and interests of your employees. Make sure that if you use an outside firm, it will allow adding some questions to the survey.

Because employees have different needs and requirements, does that mean that you need to do many different surveys such as you might need for your customers? Probably not. It is important to segment employees based upon common characteristics and priorities, but I don't think you need multiple survey instruments. Use the same basic survey with all types of employees, with a few (4 to 7) questions that may be unique to each category of employee. For example, you would probably ask some different questions of upper management from those you would ask your hourly workforce.

The generic issues that you need to ask about on any employee survey are as follows:

- Pay.
- Advancement/growth opportunities.
- Job-stress levels.
- Overall climate.

- Extent to which executives practice stated organization values.
- Benefits.
- Workload.
- Supervisor competence.
- Openness of communication.
- Physical environment/ergonomics.
- Safety.

Companies manipulate employee surveys to get good scores the same way they do with customer satisfaction surveys. They do this so they can report good news to senior management. HR typically conducts the surveys, catching the wrath of executives if morale is low. So, it's in HR's best interest to design the survey so that results are more positive.

The wording of questions and the scales used on questions should be designed to identify the extent to which you have delighted your employees, not merely satisfied them. One large corporation had a goal that 60 percent of their employees would give them a rating of 3 on a 5-point scale of overall satisfaction (1 = very dissatisfied; 5 = very satisfied). This company clearly does not care about delighting its employees; it will be achieving its goal if close to half the employees are dissatisfied with their jobs. This is another reason why it may be better to use an outside firm to do the employee survey. The outside firm has no vested interest in making the results come out well. They have also done item analyses on their survey instruments to weed out poorly worded or otherwise bad questions.

Many large corporations conduct employee morale or climate surveys once every three years, with a sample of employees. When challenged about this, they have all kinds of rationalizations as to why they do not do it more frequently. Imagine if a company only got feedback from their customers once very three years. Employees have a choice, too, and can quit at any time. Waiting until you have a mass exodus is too late to do anything about an employee morale problem. You should conduct a comprehensive employee satisfaction survey at least once a year. Pacific Bell does theirs twice a year, and some companies do surveys once a quarter.

OTHER WAYS OF MEASURING THE SOFT SIDE
OF EMPLOYEE SATISFACTION

Soft measures of employee satisfaction are measures of their opinions and feelings. Formal employee surveys are a good way of periodically taking a reading of morale levels and identifying potential problems before they get out of hand. The problem with a survey is that it gives you no depth. Surveys tell you that 60 percent of your employees are not satisfied with the company's approach to safety, for example. This gives you enough data to tell you to do more data gathering. A survey will not tell you enough to go out and begin solving a problem. Other data collection methods are used to gather more detailed data. One of the best ways of getting at this detail is focus groups of 6 to 10 employees who are called together to have a confidential discussion about a particular issue. With a skilled facilitator, a great deal of information can be brought out that will tell you exactly what the problem is and give you some clues as to how to remedy it.

Focus group data are hard to quantify, but can be done so with some imagination. I recently participated in a focus group led by a company called Business Incentives (BI). The firm made use of hand-held responders that it gave to each member of the group. These devices, which look like TV remote controls, are used to have members of the group prioritize issues or give ratings to various factors. In this case, we were identifying important topics to cover in a new training workshop that was being developed. This approach works great because it is very fast, giving immediate feedback on the overall feelings of the entire group. Every member of the group must input on each decision before totals are tabulated; no one can see how others are voting.

Another good source of soft employee satisfaction data is just talking to employees. Management by wandering around or by walking around really is a good way of taking the pulse of employee morale levels, if it is done right. If you have an atmosphere of openness and trust in your organization, and managers are skilled at getting people to open up, this approach works great. However, in my experience, most organizations do not have this trust; open communication is frequently punished. Further, many managers turn these management-by-walking-around visits into unannounced inspections that employees come to dread. I have run across a number of managers who have made this approach succeed, even in companies where there is little trust and openness. I remember talking to one executive who was a vice president in a major aerospace company who informed me that she measures morale through her weekly staff meetings. Her small staff of about 12 meet every Friday for two hours. One of the topics on the agenda each week is: "How are you feeling about your job?" Because of the respect and openness that this woman's leadership style fostered, the Friday staff meetings are actually a great way to check on employee satisfaction levels once a week.

Just as customer complaints are a good source of customer satisfaction data, so are employee complaints or grievances. Most employees, like customers, will not bother to complain, however. Often, this is because we have made it so difficult to complain. Filing a grievance is typically a time-consuming task, as is filing a written complaint. Some companies encourage employees to complain by making it simple and anonymous. Northrop Grumman has a special telephone line that employees can use to anonymously call in complaints. In the Shared Services group of Pacific Bell, executives take calls from employees once a month on any issue that they want to discuss. This helps keep executives in touch with employee satisfaction levels and gives employees an easy way to voice their concerns to upper management.

Most organizations are lean and mean today. Staff levels have been cut to the bone, and no one but the president has a secretary or assistant anymore. You can reengineer everything, but a certain amount of work won't go away. In many of the organizations I've worked with in the last few years, employees at all levels are being pushed to their limits. People are working 70 to 80 hours a week, spending 8 to 10 hours in meetings and another couple of hours a day answering voice mail and reading reports and documents. One organization came up with what it calls the employee stress index, which it calculates monthly. The stress index is made up of the following factors:

- Average number of hours worked per week by salaried and hourly employees.

- Incidence of stress-related illnesses (ulcers, high blood pressure, and so on).

- Stress-causing events in the workplace (for example, layoffs, poor financial results, and so on).

- Employee self-report measures of stress levels (collected via random telephone surveys).

- Prescriptions for stress-related drugs like Prozac or blood-pressure medication.

HARD MEASURES OF EMPLOYEE SATISFACTION

Soft measures of employee satisfaction are more preventive in nature. These data help you identify potential problems before they get too bad so that something can be done to correct them. Your organization's scorecard also has to include some hard measures of employee behavior that are related to their satisfaction levels. For example, voluntary turnover is probably a good one, if you can determine the real reasons why people are leaving. An employee who quits to go back to school or have a baby, moves because a spouse has a job in another state, or simply because another firm offers more money does not really mean that you have a morale problem. Similarly, low turnover may not be positive either. Many organizations have low turnover these days even though employees are not very happy. Having any job is surely better than no job. Measures of employees quitting because of satisfaction issues should be included in your database. The key is to get at the real reasons. Most large companies and many small and medium-sized ones conduct the obligatory exit interview; there's a spot on the form to indicate reason for leaving. Most employees lie, not wanting to burn their bridges. If you already have a better job, nothing can be gained by bad-mouthing the boss or the company, so most make up a nice generic answer: "The new company is offering me more opportunities to use the skills I have." A skilled interviewer ought to be able to get the truth with a little probing, but most don't bother— they simply write a three-word answer in the space on the form and get it over with.

Another good hard measure of employee satisfaction levels in particular facilities or departments is requests for transfer in and out. If you receive 50 requests a year from employees wanting to transfer into your department and no one has ever requested to be transferred out to another department, this is a fairly good indicator of morale levels. Of course, sometimes this may relate to the jobs in your department or location. You may have a great plant, but if its location is not ideal, then requests for transfer may not be something you can do much about.

Another hard measure that might be included in this category of your organization's metrics is employee safety. I have suggested including employee safety measures with environmental and public responsibility measures, but lost-time accidents and similar measures could just as well go in this area.

THE EMPLOYEE SATISFACTION INDEX

Ideally, all organizations should come up with an overall employee satisfaction index (ESI) that gives them one number to look at to determine employee morale levels. As with the customer satisfaction index (CSI), the ESI should be comprised of a mix of soft and hard measures that are each assigned a weight based on their importance as a predictor of employee satisfaction levels. For example, you might compute your ESI once a quarter by assigning weights to the individual metrics illustrated in Table 10.1. The approach in Table 10.1 is a good mix of metrics. It consists of about 60 percent soft measures and about 40 percent hard measures of employee behavior that are related to satisfaction levels. The hard measures are absenteeism, transfer requests, turnover, and more than half of the stress index.

HOW EXCELLENT COMPANIES MEASURE EMPLOYEE SATISFACTION

- Employees are segmented according to common needs; systematic research is done at least once a year to determine employee needs and priorities.

TABLE 10.1 Sample Employee Satisfaction Index

Climate survey	35%
Focus groups	10%
Complaints/grievances	10%
Stress index	20%
Voluntary turnover	15%
Absenteeism	5%
Transfer requests	5%
Total	100%

- Formal morale or climate surveys are conducted with large samples of employees at least once a year.

- Focus groups and other techniques are used several times throughout the year to gather qualitative data on employee satisfaction.

- Hard measures of employee satisfaction such as absenteeism and turnover are collected and reported on a regular basis (for example, monthly).

- Measures relating to employee morale focus on delighting employees rather than just satisfying them.

- Individual measures relating to employee satisfaction are summarized into an employee satisfaction index (ESI).

- Data are collected on employee satisfaction levels of other similar organizations to use for comparison and goal setting.

- Methods and instruments used to measure employee satisfaction are continually evaluated and improved.

Part III

Redesigning Your Measurement System

How to Design Your Own Measurement System

Designing your own new and improved measurement system may not be as much work as you think; it will save you much time later. In fact, organizations claim to be able to save at least a couple of hours per week that used to be wasted reviewing and trying to make sense out of meaningless data. If you figure two hours per week per technical or managerial employee times 48 weeks times the labor rate per hour, you're talking a lot of money. Of course, like most projections of this nature, it will be difficult to find these dollars on the balance sheet. A side benefit of reengineering your measurement system is that you will be making better business decisions.

TWO APPROACHES: TOP-DOWN OR BY UNIT/LOCATION

The two approaches that work when redesigning an organization's measurement system are the top–down strategy and the individual location or unit strategy. Both approaches can be very effective, depending upon the culture of your organization. If yours is an organization where corporate exerts a great deal of control, the top–down approach will obviously fit the best. This approach also has the advantage of being faster to implement, and makes it less likely that there will be "disconnects" or inconsistencies between corporate measures and those in various units or locations. The top–down approach is doomed to failure in organizations that let business units or locations maintain a great deal of autonomy. In these types of organizations, anything that is dictated from corporate is almost certain not to work.

THE TOP-DOWN APPROACH

The top–down approach works by starting with the CEO and her direct reports to develop a set of macro metrics for the entire organization. This

TABLE 11.1   Corporate Measures: Air Products and Chemicals Inc.*

Return on equity	Earnings growth
Capital reinvestment rate	Lost-time incidents and compliance with responsible care codes
Customer satisfaction	Percent international sales
Percent sales from new products	Training hours/employee
Employee morale/satisfaction	

*Reproduced with permission from Air Products and Chemicals Inc.

approach was used by Air Products and Chemicals Inc., among others. Air Products came up with a set of nine metrics that make up its corporate scorecard (see Table 11.1). By using these nine corporate metrics, each group developed its own scorecard, with some of the same measures as those of the entire corporation and some that were unique to its business. One of the largest groups in the company is the Chemicals Group. The overall metrics used to evaluate its performance are in Table 11.2.

As you can see, by comparing the corporate measures with the Chemicals Group measures, there is a great deal of consistency, but the business unit goes deeper in coming up with a more detailed set of metrics than those of the corporation.

STARTING AT THE BUSINESS UNIT OR LOCATION LEVEL

Another approach to developing a new set of measures for your organization is to begin with a single business unit or location and use it as the prototype for the rest of the organization. One organization that approached reengineering its measurement systems this way was FMC Corporation of Chicago. FMC consists of 27 fairly diverse operating divisions or business units. Like many large companies, corporate allows the business units a great deal of autonomy. Rather than dictate a set of corporate measures from which each business unit must derive its own, the corporation picked six business units to serve as prototypes for designing their own balanced scorecards. Using consultants, the four FMC divisions put together their own scorecards. The initial 4 units had so much

TABLE 11.2   Scoreboard, Chemicals Group—Air Products and Chemicals*

Health/Environmental/Safety	Sales
Compliance with responsible care codes	Percent sales growth per year
Lost-time incident rate	Dollar total sales
OSHA recordable rate	Percent international sales
Percent reduction of emissions	
Percent total waste reduction	

Profitability	Employees
Percent earnings growth	Employee satisfaction index
Dollar profit before taxes	Training hours per employee
Percent return on equity	Diversity percentages
Percent reinvestment rate	Performance vs. objectives—Plan
Dollar net income	Percent voluntary turnover
Business objectives vs. plan	

Customers	Technology
Customer satisfaction index	Percent sales from new products
Complaints/shipments	Technical service customer
Flawless execution index	satisfaction levels
Percent market share	

Productivity	Speed
Dollar profit per employee	Days to resolve complaints
Manufacturing productivity	Cycle time—product development

*Reproduced with permission from Air Products and Chemicals Inc.

success with their new scorecards that the remaining 21 business units began redesigning their own measurement systems.

A similar approach was used by Cargill, Inc.—one of the largest privately owned companies in the United States. Cargill also prefers a hands-off approach to implementing a new method for performance measurement. Cargill has always been an extremely successful company, but in the 1990s, the company decided to adapt its performance measurement to even better reflect a long-term point of view. The company also felt that it needed better measures that related to customer and employee satisfaction.

Working with Cargill for the last two years I have conducted workshops on the new performance measurements for key decision makers in the company. Many of its major business units have embraced the concepts of concentrating on a few key metrics and having balance in those measures. The key to making this work at Cargill is that none of it was forced on anyone. Attendance at the workshops was even voluntary. At first, we had trouble getting enough people in a single region to warrant holding the workshop. Once word spread that this was a valuable learning experience, we had the opposite problem, and in 1995 attendance was completely full.

During the last half of the two-day workshop, we divide the class into teams by business unit or location; they work on developing a rough draft of a set of measures for their organization. Each team documents its new set of measures, and this information is shared with all members of the workshop, so others can adopt ideas they like from other businesses. This has also worked well. Someone comes up with a unique approach to computing an overall employee satisfaction index; four or five other businesses like the approach so much, they copy it. The only problem with Cargill's approach is that the corporation is still asking for data on mostly short-term financial measures, even though many of the businesses have begun collecting data on longer-term measures such as customer and employee satisfaction. For the balanced scorecard approach to work, the whole corporation—bottom to top—needs to hold itself accountable for results in all areas of performance. The process is evolving in that direction.

PROCESS FOR REDESIGNING YOUR MEASUREMENT SYSTEM

Forming the Project Team and Getting It Trained

It should go without saying that the first task in redesigning your measurement system is to form a team. The team should consist of a cross-section of 6 to 8 individuals, who are high enough in the organization to understand the big picture and whose input will be valuable to the project. Obviously, you also need a project manager or team leader. In some companies, this has been the CEO. In others, the chief financial officer (CFO), or even the vice president of a function like quality or human resources. The job doesn't matter as much as the person. Once you've formed the team, plan a series of meetings and follow-up assignments to complete the project. It also should go without saying that all members of the team need to receive training on the concepts outlined in this book. A number of organizations conduct public workshops on the balanced-scorecard approach to measurement (for example, the Institute for International Research and the Conference Board). Based on workshops I have designed and conducted on the topic of measurement, workshops should be two to three days in length. A one-day session is just not enough.

The following is the six-step process for redesigning your measurement system:

1. Prepare guiding documents.

2. Conduct a situation analysis.

3. Define key success factors and business fundamentals.

4. Identify macro performance measures.

5. Develop a measurement plan.

6. Design data collection instruments and procedures.

Prepare Guiding Documents

The first step in redesigning your measurement system is to look at key guiding documents that establish who you are and where you want to go. I hope that you will not need to create any of these statements, but only need to review ones that already exist. If starting the project without any of these guiding documents, you can count on having a few extra three- or four-hour meetings and going through five or more drafts of these statements before everyone agrees on the words.

Different organizations have different meanings for terms like vision, mission, values, and similar terms. For the purposes of this book, I define them as follows:

MISSION: Defines who you are—your products, services, customers/ markets, and overall strengths.

VISION: Identifies where you want the organization to be in the future.

VALUES: Words or phrases that outline what the company believes in or considers important in running the business; what you stand for or consider important.

Mission Statements.

The mission statement should explain what you are and why your organization exists. The test of a good mission statement is that it should be specific enough so that it could not be applied to another organization. Therefore, it should not be vague with statements such as "a quality-focused, world-class diversified manufacturer of products that meet the real needs of our customers." You could take this statement and apply it to just about any manufacturing company. Some of the things important to mention in your mission statement that differentiate you from other similar organizations are:

- Locations
- Specific products/services
- Markets/major customers
- Classification of products/services (for example, best, lowest cost, and so on)

Because most organizations typically have an existing mission statement, do not waste time wordsmithing it if it is OK as is. I recommend asking the project team to review the mission so as to make sure that it is clear. If it is not, a separate meeting should be held to rewrite it.

Vision Statements.

The vision statement is the one guiding document that usually needs the most surgery. Chapter 12 discusses good and bad vision statements and their importance in establishing overall business strategy. One of the first things the team needs to do is review the vision statement to make sure it is clear to everyone as to where the company is going and how it will know when it gets there. As mentioned in Chapter 12, look for vague phrases and words like "leading supplier" and "world-class." Cargill's vision for the corporation is to double in size by the year 2000. This is clear to every one of the 70,000 employees in this company. With most company vision statements I've seen, if you ask 10 different employees what it means, you get 10 different answers.

Values Statements.

The third type of guiding document to look at is a statement of your values. What does the company stand for? Every organization has certain values or priorities that govern its behavior. Often these are not written down, but they are understood by all employees. In Steelcase, another very successful privately held company, one of its values is that your family and personal life come before your job in priority. Take a look at the values you have defined for your organization, and question whether or not they are really those that govern the behavior of the organization. The reason that it is important to review these guiding documents is that they will be used to help you define your key success factors and your measures in your scorecard.

Conduct a Situation Analysis

A situation analysis is typically done as part of the organization's annual or strategic planning processes. As with the guiding documents, it is hoped that this will have already been completed before you commence the measurement redesign project. A situation analysis involves researching your own strengths and weaknesses and those of your major competitors, and identifying trends that might impact your business in the next 5 to 7 years. In your vision, define where you want the organization to be in the future. The situation analysis is used to investigate factors that might prevent or help reach your destination or goal. Some of the questions that should be answered by a situation analysis are the following:

- Where do we currently stand in the market relative to our largest competitors?

- What are the major strengths, weaknesses, and strategies of our large competitors?

- What is happening with technology that might impact our business?

- What types of regulations or other outside influences could impact our organization?

- What are some current or predicted future economic or societal trends that might impact our business?

- What are our current strengths and weaknesses?

- Are we in a growing or shrinking market?

It should go without saying that a situation analysis is not done by sitting in a conference room, brainstorming answers to these questions. Go out and do some research so that your analysis is based on fact not conjecture.

Define Key Success Factors

Now comes the real work. This is the most difficult and critical step in the process. If you do a poor job defining key success factors, your measurement system is doomed to failure, and perhaps so is your organization. Before I explain how to define key success factors, it will be easier if I start by explaining what they are not. In designing measurement systems, teams often get to this step and end up with a list of poorly defined key success factors such as the following:

- Defect-free products

- Highly skilled motivated workforce

- Flexibility to adapt to changing market conditions

- Continued growth through new product development

- Delighting customers

- Partnerships with high-quality suppliers

- World-class safety record

Although these variables are important for success, they are also fairly generic. It would be difficult to find an organization whose success is not dependent upon doing these things. Key success factors should answer the question: *What do you need to do in your business to differentiate yourself from your direct competitors?* Forget the generic list of factors— it's assumed. I want to know the few things that you will focus on to differentiate yourself from everyone else in the marketplace.

The example I use in the workshops is to say that my vision is to be the next Phil Crosby. Everyone in the business world knows of Phil Crosby; he is certainly one of the most successful and probably richest management gurus to come along in a while. I ask the workshop to help me achieve my vision by identifying the factors that made Phil Crosby so successful. Someone invariably starts by saying he wrote a book. I respond that I have published several books that have sold well, but that I haven't been able to retire on the royalties yet. After a bit of discussion and guidance, the workshop attendees come up with a good list of key success factors on which to concentrate if I really want to become the next Phil Crosby or Tom Peters. The key success factors for a management consultant are as follows:

- Exposure (for example, good public relations, getting your name in print)
- Having a hook or new way of looking at an old concept (for example, reengineering or cost of quality)
- Excellent public speaking/communication skills
- Write a best-selling business book
- Experience consulting with world-class corporations
- Track record of success to build positive word of mouth
- Outstanding selling skills

Based on this list of key success factors, it seems that having a Ph.D. from a prestigious business school is not a primary prerequisite to becoming a rich and famous business consultant. Some of the other things you might expect to see atop the list are also not there. For example, how many famous management consultant are former CEOs of successful companies? Not many. What I like about the key success factors is that they identify specific variables that a management consultant would need to concentrate on to be successful. One of the reasons Phil Crosby and Tom Peters have been so successful is that they know how to market themselves. Their names are mentioned in 20 to 30 publications a month and their faces have been on many magazine covers. Public relations and exposure seem to be a key success factor, yet many consultants spend little or no money or time on this, thinking that it is unprofessional. The adage, "If you're good, people will come to you" is not entirely true. Entertainers know the importance of getting good press, and they pay big money for it. Even Dr. Steven Covey recently appeared on *Oprah*. How many book sales do you think that generated? Somebody told me that you sell an average of 10,000 copies of your book for every minute you appear on *Oprah*.

Identify Macro Performance Measures

Team members should start this step in the process by reviewing the current key performance metrics. One organization I consulted had whittled its key result measures down to 64 and could not reduce them any further. If you are in this situation, you're obviously in big trouble. In the this company's case, it threw out most of the 64 measures and started over. I hope your organization's measures are in better shape at the start. There are three process steps in this phase of the project:

1. Identify measurement categories.

2. Brainstorm measures within each category.

3. Narrow down measures to the vital few.

Identify Measurement Categories.

The first decision to make is: What categories do you want on your scorecard? Kaplan and Norton suggest that you need only four boxes:

- Customer

- Financial

- Internal

- Growth/innovation

The customer perspective includes hard measures like repeat business and on-time delivery, as well as softer measures like customer satisfaction. The financial measures are obvious—profit, ROI, ROE, and sales. Internal measures are the variables that must be controlled to achieve good performance on the other three types of measures. Internal measures often include cycle time, productivity, and safety. Growth and innovation measures relate to the factors that will help ensure the company's future. One engineering company measures the amount of time spent with customers discussing new projects, along with implemented employee suggestions, as two measures that fall in this box on the scorecard.

One of the regional Bell telephone operating companies has four boxes on its scorecard:

- Cost

- Job fulfillment

- Process improvement

- Customer satisfaction

Many of Cargill's businesses have designed scorecards that include seven categories of measures:

1. Customer satisfaction (external perspective)

2. Product/service quality (internal perspective)

3. Financial

4. Safety/environmental

5. Supplier performance

6. Employee satisfaction

7. Operational (productivity, yield, cycle time)

All three configurations work well. In my workshops, I present different classification models and allow each team to select the one it likes best. The key to having a good scorecard is not to forget your customers or employees; the scorecard should have a good mix of short- and long-term measures. The categories are only used to sort the measures and to make sure you don't leave out any important ones. Cargill wanted separate categories for employee satisfaction, supplier performance, and safety/environmental performance because of the importance of these three factors to its business.

Brainstorm Measures within Each Category.

The meeting facilitator labels a flip chart with one of the measurement categories (for example, employee satisfaction) and the team calls out possible metrics that would fall within that category. When brainstorming what could be measured, the team also lists what actually is being measured in the organization. Maximize use of existing measures as much as possible. Even if you think the metrics are flawed, list them anyway. Once the team has listed a page or two of possible metrics for one category, proceed in the same manner with the remaining categories. When you are finished, you will probably end up with 15 to 20 metrics in each of the 4 to 8 categories of data.

When brainstorming measures, make sure that the team looks at the key success factors as stimuli to help think of good measures. For example, one of the key success factors related to my goal of becoming the next Phil Crosby is good public relations. Some of the measures we might brainstorm for this key success factor are as follows:

- Number of times per month my name is mentioned in the media

- Number of times per month my name is mentioned in targeted media

- Amount of coverage per month of Mark Brown—inches of copy

- Number of citations per month of Mark Brown or his publications by other authors

- Number of features or articles per month that deal exclusively with Mark Brown's work

- Number of magazine covers that display Mark Brown's picture.

It is important to refer to the key success factors when brainstorming measures because they all must have at least one associated metric in the final scorecard. If it is something upon which your future success is dependent, you want to make sure that you measure it. Measures on your scorecard also come from considering basic business fundamentals like market share, growth, and meeting regulatory standards. Not all measures need to be derived from key success factors.

Narrow Down Measures to the Vital Few

The third and last step in the process is to narrow down the brainstormed measures to no more than 20. That means that if you have five categories of measures, you would have about four measures per category. Because you're starting out with 15 to 20 in each category, most will have to be eliminated to narrow down your list to about three to four. One way of doing this without eliminating measures is to combine them into an index. A number of examples of how to do this were provided in earlier chapters on the specific types of measures. The easiest way of taking four to six individual metrics and combining them into an index is to assign a weight to each metric based on its relative importance and compute an overall index on a scale of 0 to 10, or 0 to 100 percent. A scale of 0 to 100 percent usually works best because it allows showing small incremental changes better. Chapter 8 presents a much more detailed explanation of how to calculate an overall index.

Another way of reducing the overall number of measures is to eliminate those that are subsidiary or part of others. For example, if you are already tracking profit, you may not need income and expenses as separate metrics, because these are used to compute profit. This does not mean that you are going to eliminate any of these measures from your database. It just means that not all of the measures you have brainstormed are going to end up in your list of macro measures for the entire organization. People are always reluctant to remove any measures from their database. The 100 or so measures that have been brainstormed are probably all important metrics. However, no one can manage 100 variables. A good way of helping the team members think of the vital few is to ask them to consider the following scenario:

> You are the CEO and have gone on a three-month vacation. You are allowed to look at four (financial, customer satisfaction, or whatever category) graphs every month to tell you about the health of the company. What would you want to see on those four graphs?

To get the number of measures down to the vital few, one approach is to ask each team member to list the top four metrics individually. Each team member's top four are then listed on the flip chart to come up with which ones the group thinks are the most critical. After the measures that the group thinks are the most important are looked at, the next step is to discuss and reach consensus on the most important metrics for each category. Remember, you want a maximum of 20 measures across all categories, and 10 or 12 are even better. Therefore, if you have eight categories of data, you can only have a couple of measures in each category.

Develop a Measurement Plan

After selecting the vital few key measures, which may require several meetings, the next task is to develop a measurement plan. This involves preparing a different sheet for each of the categories in your scorecard. The measurement plan is shown in Table 11.3. The key success factors and business fundamentals are each assigned a number, so they don't have to be listed in the last column of the measurement plan.

As you can see from this table, the measures are listed along the left side of the chart according to your categories. The second column is used to specify the data collection method that will be used. If you already collect data on a particular measure, simply write: "Existing tracking system." If you do not currently collect data on this measure, identify your initial thoughts on the method that will be used. Some data collection methods include the following:

- Surveys.
- Checklists.
- Inspection.
- Analysis.
- Purchase from outside source.
- Observation.
- Focus groups.
- Laboratory testing.
- Mystery shopper.
- Counting.

The third column on the measurement plan is used to specify the frequency with which the data will be collected. The next column is optional; it is used to identify the individual in your organization who is accountable for performance on each measure. The final column is an important one, where you show the link between the measures and the key success factors and business fundamentals. *All key success factors need to have at least one associated measure in your scorecard. However, some measures may not be directly linked to a key success factor.* In other

TABLE 11.3 Measurement Plan

Measures	Data Collection Methods	Frequency	Owner	Link to Fundamental or Key Success Factor
Financial				
• Economic Value-Added (EVA)	Existing Financial Tracking	Monthly	Division President	1, 4, 8
• Cash Flow	Existing Financial Tracking	Monthly	Division President	1, 4, 8, 11
• Dollars in New Orders Booked	Sales Data Base	Weekly	V.P. Sales	11, 12
Customer				
• Market Share	• F.W. Schwartz Report	Quarterly	V.P. Marketing	3, 4, 5, 7
• Gains/Losses of Accounts	• Existing Sales Data	Monthly	V.P. Sales	3, 4, 5, 7
• Customer Value/ Satisfaction Levels	• Mail Survey	Quarterly	V.P. Marketing	3, 4, 5, 7, 11
• Price versus Competition	• Competitive Price Survey Done by Telephone	Quarterly	V.P. Marketing	5, 7, 11

155

words, it is OK to have a measure in your company database, such as profit or return on investment, that may not be linked to a key success factor. A certain number of your macro measures will be things that any business needs to measure. What is important is that the key success factors all have at least one measure, however.

Design Data Collection Instruments and Procedures

This is the part of the project that will take the most time; it also may require you to spend money on outside resources. Using the data collection methods identified in the previous step, you need to first ask the question: Can we use existing data collection instruments and methods? For example, if you are currently surveying customers every quarter to determine their satisfaction levels, you may want to continue using these existing surveys, or possibly modify them. After reviewing all of the final measures in your scorecard, the team should make a list of measures for which no data collection methods and procedures currently exist. Typically, this is about 50 to 60 percent of the scorecard. Next, you need to decide on the overall strategy for acquiring the data collection instruments and procedures. Some things are better to farm out to experts and other data are better collected yourself. It is often less expensive to purchase the data collection services from the outside. For example, employee climate or morale surveys typically cost about $5 per employee for data collection and tabulation. You may be able to design and administer your own survey less expensively, but the responses will not be as anonymous and you will be unable to compare your results with those of benchmarks and other similar companies.

During this phase of the measurement design project, the team should prepare a matrix that looks like Table 11.4. The table shows a portion of the overall planning and decision making that would have to be done regarding the design or purchase of data collection instruments and procedures. After making major decisions about the data collection methods that require new instruments and procedures to be designed or purchased, each individual project manager has to develop a project plan that details the specifications and approach that will be used. In our example table, one of the items that would have to be purchased is an employee satisfaction survey. The project plan might look the one shown in Table 11.5.

Separate project plans like the one in the table would be prepared for each measurement instrument that has to be developed or purchased from

TABLE 11.4   Data Collection Instruments and Procedures

Measure	Data Exists?	Use As Is?	Make/Buy?	Project Manager
Employee-Related				
Turnover	Yes	Yes	N/A	N/A
Employee satisfaction survey	No	N/A	Buy	J. Springer
Employee stress index	No	N/A	Make	F. Toomy
Financial				
Economic value-added	No	N/A	Make	A. Wayne
Sales dollars	Yes	Yes	N/A	N/A
Revenue growth	Yes	Yes	N/A	N/A
Operational				
Cycle time	No	N/A	Make	B. Billings
EVA/employee	No	N/A	Make	B. Billings

TABLE 11.5   Example Project Plan—Purchasing an Employee Satisfaction Survey

Task	Responsible	Schedule
1. Write specifications for employee survey	J. S.	Feb. 1
2. Write RFQ	J. S.	Feb. 1
3. Review specifications and RFQ	Meas. Team	Feb. 10
4. Identify three survey vendors and send RFQ	A. C.	Feb. 16
5. Review proposals	J. S., A. C., J. T.	Mar. 21
6. Lead meeting to select survey vendor	J. S.	Mar. 22
7. Implement survey in pilot location	Vendor and J. S.	Apr. 15
8. Lead meeting to review pilot findings	Vendor and J. S.	Apr. 30
9. Develop implementation plan for entire organization	Vendor	Apr. 15
10. Administer survey in entire organization	Vendor	May 10
11. Review results and modify instrument and methodology	Vendor and J. S.	June 1

an outside source. At this point in the project, the team that designed the overall measurement system typically has quarterly or monthly progress review meetings, where project managers report on the status of their projects associated with the measurement system.

TIME ESTIMATES FOR THE ENTIRE PROJECT

The calendar time needed to complete the entire project typically ranges from six months to a year. Each member of the team typically attends four to six half-day meetings and another four to six 2-hour meetings during the course of the project. Total time commitment for meetings, therefore, is 24 to 36 hours. An additional couple of days is usually spent attending training on the balanced-scorecard approach to measurement. Each team member also typically spends three to six days doing work outside of team meetings to develop measurement systems and procedures. The total time an individual might spend in the course of a year-long project is around 8 to 12 days. The team leader will spend about 25 percent more time than team members.

The amount of time required for the project is directly related to how bad your current measurement system is. If you have to throw it away and start over from scratch, it could take two or more years to complete the measurement redesign project. This is not usually the case, however. Most organizations implement this approach within four to six months of their initial training and the formation of a project team.

For more information on the approach to designing a new scorecard for your company, I highly recommend a Harvard Business School video called *Measuring Corporate Performance: The Balanced Scorecard* (1994).

Linking Measures to Strategy and Key Success Factors

Today's managers recognize the impact that measures have on performance. But they rarely think of measurement as an essential part of their strategy.

—Robert S. Kaplan and David P. Norton

It has become quite fashionable for organizations today to develop vision and mission statements and a list of values. Somehow, they think that these carefully chosen words will become a magic mantra that will help the company achieve world-class levels of performance. In my experience, most of these companies have wasted a lot of time and money coming up with mission and vision statements. The executives hire a consultant for a couple of days and they all go off to a resort and spend two days drafting a couple of paragraphs that make up the organization's mission and vision statements. The mission says who we are; the vision says who we want to be. If you look at 20 to 30 mission and vision statements, as I have, you will be amazed at how similar they are, even though the organizations to which they pertain are quite different from each other. It's as if someone got out the jargon generator and threw these things together. Some of the words and phrases you tend to see in many of these statements are as follows:

- World-class.
- Competitive.
- Real needs of customers.
- Benchmark level.
- Integrate.

- Innovative.

- Profitable.

- Cost-effective.

- Value-added.

- Targeted customers.

- Customer-focused.

- Market-driven.

The executives come back from their retreat, mission and vision statements in hand, and display them all over the organization. The mission and vision statements are promoted with a great degree of fanfare, as if words by themselves will somehow transform the company. The mission and vision are put onto plaques, published in newsletters, and communicated using a variety of media and methods. One company even programmed all the computer terminals so that when employees signed on in the morning, the mission and vision appeared on the initial screen. It also gave every employee a marble paperweight with a bronze plaque that had the mission and vision engraved on it. Employees referred to this as the "mission and vision brick." In spite of all this communication, not one employee out of about 50 I interviewed could tell me the mission and vision off the top of their heads.

Another company did a better job of communicating the mission, vision, and values. It used all of the typical communication methods and gave each employee a wallet card with the information printed on it. Managers throughout the company asked everyone to use the card to memorize the mission, vision, and values. To encourage this to happen, they made little games out of it. During training sessions, employees had to put together puzzles whose pieces consisted of the components of the mission statement. Or managers in the plants would walk through the work areas and quiz employees on the mission and vision. Employees who could recite the statements without looking at their wallet cards received a coupon for a free lunch. Those who had their wallet cards but couldn't remember the words at least got a free beverage. After all this effort of getting employees to memorize the words, did the company culture or performance change? Not at all. A survey done later revealed that more than two-thirds of the employees believed that the mission and vision did not drive performance in the company and that management behavior was inconsistent with the company's stated values.

WHY MISSION AND VISION STATEMENTS DON'T WORK

Developing mission and vision statements will do nothing to change or improve your organization unless other changes follow. Many organizations are frustrated when they spend time and money developing these statements and performance fails to improve. In a videotape by Kaplan and Norton called *Measuring Corporate Performance,* the CEO of an engineering and undersea construction company called Rockwater explains the frustration of employees failing to see how the company mission and vision translated into their jobs. People understood where the company needed to go in the future, but they did not understand how they could contribute to the vision. In his book *Vital Signs* (New York: AMACOM Press, 1993) Arthur Andersen consultant Steve Hronec explains:

> Management spends a lot of time developing mission statements, but often gets diverted from the details of developing a set of performance measures. (p. 3)

Why is it that this seems to occur so frequently? It is because developing a set of measures is difficult and often boring work. Executives like to do the big macro thinking characterized by such work as developing vision statements. They don't like to get down in the trenches and work on mundane tasks like developing measures and data collection methods. They often don't understand that without this link their vision will never be realized. They make speeches about the mission and vision, and how important they are, and then go out and ask for short-term financial results. They talk about the importance of innovation and long-term thinking, and then ask for quarterly financial results. As an outsider, it seems so obvious why companies struggle with achieving their mission and vision, but I guess these inconsistencies are tough to see from the inside.

Another common problem with vision statements is that employees cannot relate to them. The statements focus on being the biggest and best, or on making the most money for shareholders, and they contain nothing about the employees or how they are involved in the future destination of the organization. Some employees don't support the vision statements because they don't understand them; some don't support them because they don't understand their role in helping the company reach its vision. Some vision statements focus directly on obliterating the competition; they seem mean-spirited to employees. For example, one of the visions of a large credit card company is to "Put American Express out of business."

AT&T takes a different tack with its vision. Rather than concentrate on capturing specific markets or putting competitors out of business, AT&T's vision states that the company is "Dedicated to becoming the world's best at bringing people together—giving them easy access to each other and to the information and services they want and need—anytime, anywhere." This is one of the best written vision statements that I have seen. It is clear, specific, and presents a message without the use of jargon. AT&T requires executives to operationalize words such as "anytime, anywhere" into specific performance measures and goals to help ensure that the vision is not just nice-sounding words on paper.

DEVELOPING STRATEGY

The key to having a good measurement system is to have a good strategy. Measures need to be derived from your strategy and from an analysis of the key business factors you need to concentrate on to ensure that you achieve your vision. Every successful company has a well-thought-out strategy. A strategy is how you are going to provide some product or service in such a way that customers will prefer dealing with your company rather than with your competitors. Federal Express is one company whose success has been built around a well-thought-out strategy. Chairman Fred Smith found a strategy that would allow his company to provide on-time delivery of overnight packages anywhere in the country. In 1973, Federal Express was the only company offering this service, and its sales grew and grew as demand increased. Others tried to copy Federal Express's approach/strategy, but offer the same service for less money. It turned out that a cheaper rate for a package often meant that it did not get there the next day. Twenty some years later, Federal Express still has a good strategy, and it still provides the best service in the industry.

Having one good strategy may not be enough to carry through the next 10 or 20 years, however. Competitors can usually copy your strategy and often provide the same product or service for a lower cost. The Baby Bells are all of a sudden lowering fees for residential phone service now that they will have to compete for that business. Pizza Hut decided to take a slice of Domino's business by offering delivery service. United Airlines' new Shuttle business unit is set up to compete directly with Southwest, with its low fares and no-frills service. United's strategy is to offer the same low fares with a higher caliber of service, such as assigned seats.

THE KEY TO A SOUND STRATEGY

According to C. K. Prahalad and Gary Hamel's groundbreaking article ("The Core Competencies of the Corporation," *Harvard Business Review*, May/June 1990), the key to a sound business strategy is to *do something that others cannot do, or do something well that others do poorly, or have great difficulty doing well.* These are characteristics of all successful organizations.

The difficult part is finding that one thing you can do better than anyone else, and not letting competitors copy your strategy. Southwest Airlines' strategy for success allowed it to provide cheaper fares to customers and deliver higher profits than their competitors. Their strategy of no-frills service and quick turnaround at the gates became well-known among other airlines. United's Shuttle service is an attempt to copy directly many parts of Southwest's strategy and add a few twists to make it appear superior to its customers. For example, one of the things that I always hate about flying Southwest is that the later you arrive at the gate, the worse your seat is. Because it has no assigned seats, all the best seats are taken by passengers who get to the gate early. United's Shuttle service offers the same low fares and frequent flights as Southwest, but it offers assigned seats. Given the choice, many business travelers prefer United, because they can get a good seat without having to get to the airport an hour before the flight.

LINKING VISION, GOALS, STRATEGIES, AND MEASURES

Strategy comes out of your vision. Your vision should say what you want to be in 5 or 10 years. Your strategy should articulate in general terms how you will achieve your vision. Once you've identified your vision and key strategies or goals, you need to define key success factors. These are things that will need to happen for you to realize your vision and goals or strategies. Out of your goals, strategies, and vision come your performance measures.

IDENTIFYING KEY SUCCESS FACTORS

Key success factors are the things that you need to do or the capabilities you need to have to achieve your goals and vision. Key success factors usually have to do with things like the following:

- Competitive pricing.
- Technical capabilities.
- Growing market share.
- Improving profits.
- Investing in new equipment.
- Customized offerings.
- New products/services.
- Capacity.
- Improving quality.
- Controlling supplier quality.
- Reducing new product
  development time.
- Targeted marketing.

To get a group to identify key success factors, start by asking the question: "What are we going to need to do to achieve this vision and these long-term goals we have set for ourselves?"

Identifying key success factors is not something to be done in an hour or two with a committee of executives. It takes thought and the right data to determine exactly what is going to be necessary to succeed in the future. You need to gather data about the following to do an effective job of identifying critical success factors:

- Projections of future customers and markets.
- Strategies, strengths, and weaknesses of key competitors.
- Projections about changes in requirements and priorities of existing customers.

- Evaluation of how new technologies may impact your business.

- Research, testing, and projections of new products/services.

- Regulatory trends that may impact the organization.

- Economic and societal trends that may impact the business or organization.

- Analysis of your own strengths and weaknesses.

Taking all of these factors into considerations, executives in your organization develop a list of 8 to 12 critical factors that will impact the organization's future success and survival. Typically, a list of 30 to 50 factors are brainstormed, combined, prioritized, and narrowed down to a more manageable number such as 10 to 12.

The example in Table 12.1 shows how a hypothetical paper company defined its vision and critical success factors. As you can see from the example, this paper company has defined a vision statement that is fairly specific. It includes actual numbers for what it wants to achieve in market share. This is certainly not necessary. Vision statements are often vague. The goals are used to get more specific. Goals articulate the specific accomplishments that will be necessary to achieve the vision. Sometimes

TABLE 12.1   Example of Vision and Critical Success Factors: Paper Manufacturing Company

---

Vision: Be the preferred lowest-cost, highest-quality supplier of environmentally friendly newsprint for customers in major cities across North America, with at least 35% of the market in the United States and 25% of the markets in Mexico and Canada.

Critical Success Factors

Offer customers newsprint that contains a higher percentage of recycled paper than any of our major competitors.

Maintain our current position as being among the best 25% in the marketplace for competitive pricing.

Be viewed by customers as a supplier that is flexible and easy to do business with.

Offer customers just-in-time delivery to minimize their inventory costs.

Become ISO-9000-certified in all of our plants/mills.

---

goals are also vague. It would have been OK for the paper company to list goals such as the following:

- Increase domestic and international market share.

- Achieve preferred supplier status from major customers.

- Maintain acceptable profit levels.

The critical success factors that the paper company has listed are the things that the company will need to do—its strategies—to reach its goals and achieve its vision.

DERIVING MEASURES FROM GOALS AND SUCCESS FACTORS

The key to a sound measurement system is to avoid disconnects among measures, goals, and key success factors. This is actually quite common because these are often developed independently of each other. Whatever you have identified as a critical factor for your long-term success should be covered somehow in your overall scorecard. For example, one company identified competitive pricing as being one of its most important success factors. Yet, this company had no goals relating to pricing and no measure of pricing in its macro performance measures. Another company mentioned repeat business from existing customer accounts as critical to its long-term success. Again, no measure could be found of repeat business. An even more common error is to identify key employee competencies as a critical success factor but fail to include any measure of employee competencies in the company's overall scorecard.

Often, it is very easy to derive good measurement indices from goals and success factors. For example, if increasing market share in Pacific Rim countries is a key goal, the measure is the percentage of the market you have from these countries. Other times, you need to put a little thought into coming up with a good measurement index based around your goals and success factors. One cellular telephone network company identified flexibility in rate plans as a key success factor. The company found that it drove the wrong performance by just measuring the number of different rate plans offered. The number of rate plans was not the issue. From the customers' perspective, what they cared about is if the company had a rate plan that fit their individual needs. Adding multiple rate plans also increased administrative and selling costs, negatively impacting profits. The company developed a flexibility index that was comprised of a number of individual indices, including the number of rate plans offered, customer feedback on how well the company tailored the rate plan to its needs, and other factors.

DECEIVING MEASURES

Linking measures to key success factors seems rather simplistic, and it seems unlikely that even a moderately successful business would not have done this. The trick comes in making sure that the measures you select are actually predictive of your ability to achieve your vision and goals. At first glance, many measurement indices seem to be good ones; they appear to be connected to key success factors. However, closer examination may reveal that a measure drives performance that is contrary to the vision and goals. In Chapter 2, I talked about how a fast-food chain specializing in chicken uses a scrap measure called "chicken efficiency" to help ensure that restaurant workers don't cook too much chicken that has to be thrown away because it sits too long under the heat lamps. The performance that this measure often drives is to not cook any chicken, which means that customers have to wait 15 to 20 minutes for the chicken to be prepared. Thus, a measure that relates to saving money makes these restaurant chains look good in the short run, but chicken efficiency is a measure that may result in increases in lost customers. Many who have to wait enough times for their chicken will simply never come back, even though they like the product.

Controlling the cost of the food is certainly a key success factor for any fast-food business, so it would seem that measures like chicken efficiency are in fact linked to business strategy and key success factors. The problem is not the measure; the problem is the importance placed on it. If employees and management believe that short-term, cost-related measures are more important than longer-term measures like gains and losses of customers, this will guide their behavior. No one had been told that chicken efficiency is more important than customer service or customer retention. However, somehow the message had reached employees and managers because of how often data on chicken efficiency were asked for and reviewed by management.

MEASURES AND VALUES

Linking measures with business strategy and goals is not nearly as difficult as making sure that measures are consistent with your organization's stated values. Values are statements of what the organization believes in and the principles by which it would like to operate. Values often include open communication, creating value for shareholders, respect for the individual, integrity, providing a safe work environment, delighting customers, innovation/risk-taking, and so on. Values are just as important as having a clear vision, as Bartlett and Ghoshal explain ("Changing the Role of Top Management," *Harvard Business Review,* November/December 1994): "It's fine to stress what to aim for, but people also need to know what a company stands for."

It is important to have some way of measuring the extent to which the company actually operates according to its stated values. Many of these value statements are nothing more than rhetoric. The values on the wall talk about integrity, and open and honest communication, whereas senior management directs others to buy expensive personal gifts for clients to help ensure their future business and to keep quiet about upcoming plant closures and other actions that threaten job security. Organizations that truly want to live by the values they have on their walls have found ways of measuring their progress toward this. Values are soft and fuzzy; performance measures are usually hard and quantifiable. Inevitably, the hard quantifiable stuff gets the attention, often at the expense of the softer measures. The sentiment that I hear from employees in many of these companies is something like this:

> Sure we have values: Ethics, concern for the environment, respect for employees, quality, delighting customers, and a couple more I can't remember. That's what's on the wall; I'll tell you what is the only real value that matters: profits, profits, profits. We do whatever it takes to ensure that we always look good on the bottom line, regardless of how we achieve it.

So, how do companies ensure that their performance measures and goals don't ignore their values? They do so through the use of a balanced approach to measurement discussed throughout this book. By having measures for each executive and each employee that concentrate on employees, customers, and the community, as well as shareholders, this balance can be achieved, and a company can ensure that it operates according to its stated values. Two companies that do this well are Corning and Federal Express, both winners of the Malcolm Baldrige Award. One of Federal Express's stated values is that a manager works for his or her people, not the other way around. Fed Ex operationalizes this by requiring that each manager be evaluated by his/her employees. If employees consistently rate the boss below standard, the boss not only gets a poor score in this area, but may receive zero bonus. Even if a manager's financial performance is outstanding, she also has to achieve a good score from customers and from employees in order to be eligible for a bonus.

In his vision to turn around Corning, CEO Jamie Houghton frequently used the phrase "world-class." Houghton talked about the vision of Corning becoming one of the most respected companies in the world. Sounds nice, but how would you know if you got there? The measure Corning selected was being picked by *Fortune* magazine in its annual poll of America's most admired corporations. The poll is done by surveying top executives in the country's largest companies, and Houghton believed that it would be a good measure of how far Corning had come in its quest to become "world-class."

Reporting and Analyzing Performance Data

A great many people in business think that measuring a problem is tantamount to solving it. If measurement alone changed behavior, there would be no fat people, no one would smoke, and everyone would exercise, because all of these behaviors and their results can be easily measured.

—Aubrey C. Daniels

Fixing your measurement system by itself is not a magic bullet that will solve all of your organization's ills. No single change initiative or program will immediately transform your company from being mediocre to being world-class. Coming up with a good balanced set of performance metrics will save many hours of wasted time and make it more likely that you keep your organization on track in its journey toward reaching its vision and long-term goals. During the last five years, I have seen a number of organizations that have done a major overhaul to their measurement systems, eliminating unnecessary measures, and concentrating on adding longer-term measures like sales from new products and delighting customers. Even organizations with good balanced scorecards often have problems with reporting the data and even more problems in analyzing the data to make good business decisions.

WHAT'S IMPORTANT WHEN REVIEWING DATA

When reviewing data, it's important to remember three words:

1. Level
2. Trend
3. Variability

Level has to do with how good your performance in the most recent period is when compared to:

- Goals

- Past performance

- Competitors' performance

- Benchmark organizations

In order to evaluate level, one needs to have lots of comparative data.
When looking at any statistic, a good manager will look at the most recent data point and ask: "How are we doing compared to our goal, last
month, last year, our competition; and how do our results compare with
those of world-class companies?" Trend is the next important dimension
to examine. Trend involves looking at multiple data points over time.
Trends are either improving, getting worse, or flat. In order to evaluate
trends, you need to have enough data points. Statisticians suggest a minimum of seven data points to demonstrate a trend. The third dimension
that should be examined is variability or fluctuations in the trends and
levels of performance over time. Anomalies or dramatic increases or decreases in performance levels are important to note and have explained:
"What happened the week of August 15th; why did our productivity drop
so severely?"

COMMON PROBLEMS WITH DATA REPORTING APPROACHES
Data Are Reported in Tables Rather Than Graphs

Managers and technical professionals claim they spend a major chunk of
time each week reviewing and analyzing performance data. A lot of that
time is spent trying to decipher hard-to-read charts and tables, looking for
meaningful statistics. Most performance data that I see in companies are
reported in tables that present multiple columns of figures. I often sit next
to executives on airline flights and see them reading performance charts
with seven or eight columns of figures per page, printed in 6- or 8-point
type. It's not surprising that I often see their eyes glaze over as they start
to fall asleep while trying to make sense out of these reams of boring tables and charts. Managers in many organizations do not even use much of

the performance data they receive because they are too difficult to read and analyze. A graph is always a better way of presenting data. Graphs also typically provide information on levels, trends, and variability, information more difficult to pull out of a table of statistics.

No Comparative Data Are Presented

A practice that is extremely prevalent is to report data without any goals or comparative statistics. Data without a goal or comparison are meaningless. If I told you that your triglicerides were at a level of 150, that information is meaningless, unless I also told you that anything more than 150 is considered to be a big health problem. Even if managers and staff members are expected to know goals and desired levels of performance for each performance measure, it is still helpful to have this information on the graph for reference. In fact, I prefer actually drawing the goal on the graph right next to the actual performance data. Many organizations set goals to make themselves look good, as I will explain in the next chapter. Because of this, it is also important to have other reference points for use in evaluating levels of performance. Two obvious points of reference would be: How do our competitors perform on this metric? How do benchmark companies perform?

Only the Most Recent Data Are Reported

Most management reports show only data from this year. Data are typically reported on a monthly basis for only the months in the current year. The columns typically show performance by month, and perhaps year-to-date statistics. Having data from only the most recent time period makes it difficult to determine trends over time. With many performance measures, it is important to look at changes in trends over a long period of time. This is particularly true with measures that are only collected quarterly or perhaps less often. For example, customer satisfaction data might only be collected once a quarter, and employee satisfaction may only be measured once or twice a year.

Data Are Reported Unnecessarily

It's rare to see a management performance report that is less than a quarter-inch thick. Some are so thick they come in a 2-inch binder each month. It's little wonder they rarely are looked at. The point of this book is that every employee, from individual contributors up to the CEO, ought to be responsible for 10 to 20 measures of performance—no more. This means that no one should need a report that is longer than 20 pages. All the backup data that are often reported should be on a requested-as-needed basis or put on the company's computer database so a particular chart or figure can be called up when necessary. If performance on the overall metric is good, one does not need to see the charts on the backup or subsidiary measures.

NORTHROP GRUMMAN: THE BENCHMARK FOR REPORTING PERFORMANCE DATA

Los Angeles–based Northrop Grumman has done a lot of work in recent years to reengineer its measurement system. Northrop's acquisitions of Grumman and Vought in 1994 refocused the measurement reengineering effort, and work is still ongoing to come up with the vital few key metrics that can be used to assess all business units. One thing it has done in the last two years that has helped immensely is to standardize the format used to report performance data throughout the corporation. It used to have almost as many reporting formats as performance metrics. Even within a single business unit like the B-2 Division, one could find 20 or more different report formats in different functions and levels.

It became difficult to interpret performance data because everyone presented results in a different format. At the Military Aircraft Systems Division, a team was chartered to develop a standardized reporting method. There was concern that even if one could interpret a chart, rarely could the level of performance against benchmarks be assessed. The product of the team's effort is a standardized format for presenting performance data that is the best I've seen in any company. An example of one of its reports is shown in Figure 13.1. As you can see, it tells you everything you need to know to determine, level, trends, and variability. This figure provides more information than many 20-page performance reports I've seen. The best features of this format is that it includes annual goals, longer-term goals, and benchmark data to use in comparing current performance. It also requires the plotting of the current year's performance by month and past year's performance by year. This allows managers to identify problems early on so they can be solved. The format is also incredibly easy to read. By always having the same information in the same place every time, managers have been conditioned to look in the upper right-hand cor-

FIGURE 13.1   Northrop Grumman Performance Data Report

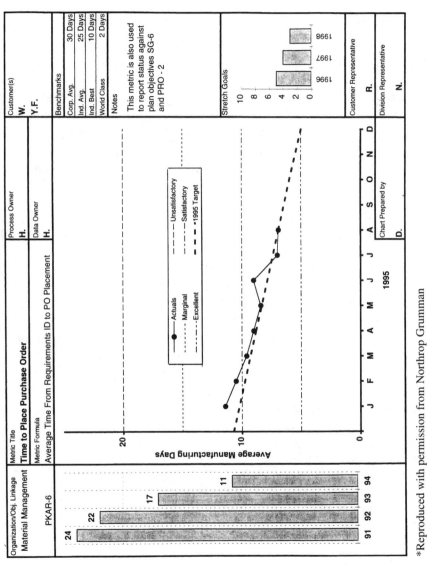

175

ner for benchmark data and the lower right-hand corner for stretch goals. Although it would be difficult to calculate, I'm sure that the standardization of metrics reporting has saved the company hundreds of thousands of dollars in management time, as well as quite a few trees.

OPEN-BOOK MANAGEMENT: TEACHING ALL EMPLOYEES TO UNDERSTAND PERFORMANCE MEASURES

An exciting trend in a number of medium and small companies is an approach to reporting performance data called *open-book management.* The approach involves sharing company financials and other key statistics with all employees. According to author John Case (*Open Book Management,* New York: Harper Business School Press, 1995), open-book management can help companies be more competitive by having all employees understand how the company makes money and how they can contribute to the company's overall performance. Implementing open-book management requires more than simply making and distributing more copies of the monthly performance reports. Employees need to be taught how to understand the performance data and be able to explain how their performance impacts the measures on the scorecard.

Effectively communicating the scorecard data to employees may involve standardizing reporting formats, as Northrop Grumman has done, or it may involve the use of creative graphics or even games to communicate the results. The Springfield Remanufacturing Company (SRC) has become the best-known open-book-management success story. Hundreds of executives visit SRC each year to learn how the company teaches employees to play the great game of business. CEO Jack Stack has become the guru of open-book management; his company has been one of the most impressive testimonials for the logic behind sharing all business information with employees.

UNDERSTANDING THE RELATIONSHIPS AMONG THE MEASURES ON YOUR SCORECARD

The most advanced companies today cannot only tell you what it means when performance on one of their key metrics changes; they can tell you exactly how performance on one measure impacts performance on others. These are the types of relationships that need to be understood to make good data-based business decisions. Most organizations I work with intuitively understand some of the relationships among different metrics, but have no hard data.

One company that has done an excellent job in this area is IBM. IBM has done research, for example, that tells it the correlation between its overall customer satisfaction measure (called net satisfaction index, NSI) and increased revenue for the corporation. Its research indicates that every 1-point increase on the 100-point NSI scale is worth $5 million to IBM in increased revenue! Individual business units can then calculate the value to them of increasing their own NSI score by determining their overall contribution to the size of the entire corporation. I have found very few organizations that have done the type of research that IBM has done to show the correlation between customer satisfaction and financial performance. Understanding relationships like this is extremely important. A proposal to spend $2 million to increase customer satisfaction by 3 points on its NSI scale would be a good investment—a 3-point increase on the NSI scale will lead to $15 million in increased revenue, a fairly good return for a $2 million investment.

Everyone talks about how important quality and customer satisfaction are these days, and most companies measure them. However, few really know how to achieve them or what achieving them will do to business. Understanding how all the measures in your scorecard impact each other is an important key to success. I worked with a chemical company that spent several years and hundreds of thousands of dollars to improve its service to customers. Because its products were mostly commodities, and its prices were about the same as everyone else's, it decided to differentiate itself from the competition by having better service. Service did improve significantly over previous levels, but it ended up not helping the company become more successful. Even though its data showed significant improvements, customers perceived its service to be about the same as the competitors' service. The improvements in service also did not lead to an increase in revenue, repeat business, or market share. The lesson to learn here is you need to know early how improvements on one type of measure might impact performance on the other metrics in your scorecard. Improving customer satisfaction, employee satisfaction, and product/service quality all frequently cost money. It's important to be able to predict how improvements in these metrics will lead to improvements in other measures like profit, market share, and increased value of the organization, as measured by indices like stock price.

THE BIG BALANCING ACT

Running a business or any type of organization is something like being a juggler. The key to success is to achieve that perfect balance of performance levels on all the different measures in your scorecard. If one goes out of whack, care must be taken not to change too drastically to get performance back in line, because it may cause problems down the road. An employee morale problem arises because of lack of career opportunities for technical professionals, so you create a technical career ladder. Three years later, you find that too many people have reached the top rungs of the ladder and your labor costs are out of sight.

Having a good solid set of metrics that provides a picture of past and projected future performance will do wonders to make your organization more successful, but by itself is not enough. Performance data are only information. If the information is not understood or correctly acted on, it won't help your organization improve. Being able to correctly analyze the data and use them to make good decisions are the essence of performance management.

14

Linking Measures, Goals, and Plans

When I turned 30, I started thinking more about my health and overall fitness level, so I decided to get some base-line data on how unhealthy I was. I never exercised, had a terrible diet, smoked, and got winded climbing a few flights of stairs. I didn't look fat, but my waist was only about 4 inches smaller than my chest. I went to a doctor as well as a personal fitness trainer and got a base-line assessment of a number of key measures of my health:

- Blood chemistry: cholesterol, glucose, and so on.

- Heart rate.

- Blood pressure.

- Respiration.

- Body fat percentage.

- Weight.

- Measurements.

- Strength.

- Flexibility.

Looking at the data was enough to shock me into action; I took some immediate steps like quitting smoking and beginning to exercise, which had a positive impact on a number of the measures. Other life-style changes took much longer to acquire, but in the years since my 30th birthday, I have gradually implemented a number of life-style changes that have allowed me to dramatically impact my levels on all of the measures listed. Achieving my vision of becoming a much healthier person required extensive reading; coaching from various doctors, nutritionists, and trainers; and a certain amount of trial-and-error experimentation with diet, exercise, and nutritional supplement strategies to hit on the formula that worked best for me.

The point of this story is that achieving your vision requires much more than having a good set of measures. You need to set short- and long-term goals for each of your measures and develop and test strategies for achieving your goals. As mentioned earlier, the phrase "You get what you measure" is a fallacy. Having a good set of measures is only the foundation of an effective renewal effort. This chapter addresses how to use your new scorecard to develop goals and strategies for achieving your vision.

MEASURES WITHOUT GOALS ARE WORTHLESS

Finding out that your cholesterol level is 250 is meaningless data unless you know that a good level of cholesterol is less than 180 and that over 300 is a heart attack waiting to happen. Every measure in your scorecard needs to have associated annual and longer-term goals. For some measures, you might even want to set monthly or quarterly goals. It is important to have shorter-term milestone goals because these enable employees to see progress and to celebrate smaller accomplishments. People have trouble sticking with long-term projects or goals, unless they can track their progress along the way and feel a sense of accomplishment for reaching key milestones.

GOALS, OBJECTIVES, AND TARGETS

Different organizations have different words they use for goals. For some, goals are the vague statements of where they want to be in the future. For these companies, the goals are almost an extension of the vision statement. A goal might be: "Become a leading supplier of gaskets and seals to the U.S. auto industry." For other companies, goals are specific levels of performance that are tied to the measures. For example, "Achieve 15 percent return on investment." Other companies call these objectives or targets. It really doesn't matter what terminology you use. *In this book, I am using the word "goal" to mean the measurable, desired level of performance for a particular measure. A goal always has two parts: the measure itself and the desired level of performance.*

Some example goals are:

- Reduce voluntary turnover to a level of 7 percent per year

- Achieve a score of 98/100 on the annual safety audit

- Reduce product defects to 30 per 10,000

- Ninety percent of our customers will rate their satisfaction with our service a "5" on a 5-point scale

Notice that with each one of these examples, we specify the measure (for example, turnover) and the desired level (7 percent) of performance. Many goals also have a time component, which is fine. We could take the third goal and add a time component to have it read: "Achieve a level of 30 defects per 10,000 products by the end of the third quarter." Goals can cover a brief time period, such as next month, or you can have longer-term goals that cover a time period of 5 or more years.

Goals need to be set at each level in the organization in a cascading fashion, so that achievement of lower-level goals leads to achievement of macro goals. As you go lower in the organization, goals tend to be based more on projects, process measures, or activities, as well as on output measures. This is fine as long as you can show the connections between process or activity goals and macro output goals.

MISTAKES ORGANIZATIONS MAKE WHEN SETTING GOALS

I spend a lot of time looking at the strategic plans of many small and large organizations during any given year. Most do a terrible job of setting goals. The five most common problems I've seen with goals are as follows:

1. Goals that are really projects, activities, or strategies.

2. Goals that are solely based on past performance.

3. Arbitrary stretch goals.

4. Inconsistent short- and longer-term goals.

5. Inconsistencies in goals at different levels of the organization.

Goals That Are Really Projects, Activities, or Strategies

This is one of the most common errors I see in organizations' strategic business plans. Many have been setting goals like this for 20 years, since they first learned about management by objectives in the 1970s. A goal should tell you what level of performance you want to see on a particular measure. It should not specify how you will achieve the level of performance. *The easiest way of making sure that your goals are not strategies or projects is to make sure that each one specifies one of the key measures in your scorecard.*

A goal that I see a lot lately is: "Achieve ISO 9000 certification by the end of the year." The problem with this goal statement is that ISO certification is typically not one of a company's key performance metrics. If it was, then this goal would be fine. Some other activity-based or strategy goals I've seen recently are as follows:

- Implement flextime in our corporate office by the end of 1996.

- Complete construction of the Knoxville plant by the third quarter of 1997.

- Have at least 50 percent of our data processing services performed by outside firms by the end of this year.

All of these three examples seem like important and meaningful activities that will help the organization improve. However, they are all projects or activity goals. You first need to set goals for the major output measures in your scorecard, and then you can set subgoals that might look like the examples that specify things you will need to do to accomplish the macro goals. For example, one key measure might be an employee satisfaction index, and a long-term goal of 80 percent employee satisfaction. Implementing flextime by the end of the year might be one of the activities to complete in order to help improve employee satisfaction levels.

Goals That Are Solely Based on Past Performance

Another common mistake I see in goal setting is to assign the level of performance in a goal based on how we did last year. This is another practice that become popular in the 1970s with the spread of management by objectives (MBO); it persists today in many places. You look at how you performed last year and set the goal 5 or 10 percent higher for this next year. One executive I talked to about this practice explained the "MBO game" played in many companies:

> The trick is to set your goals high enough so that your boss will think that you have to hustle to reach them, but low enough so that you're certain you can easily achieve the goals early in the year, and coast for the rest of the year. Hold back on reporting early achievement of the goal, however, or the boss will raise it in the middle of the year.

Organizations have been playing this MBO goal-setting game for almost as long as they have been playing the budget game, in which you ask for 20 percent more than you really need, knowing you will need to trim that much out before the budget is approved.

The problem with setting goals strictly based on past performance is that a number of organizations have five- or ten-percented themselves right out of business. Whereas they were improving by 5 percent each year, some of their competitors improved by 100 percent and stole their market share. Witness the wake-up call American car companies received when the quality of Japanese cars far exceeded their own quality levels.

Past performance is a helpful reference point when looking at setting goals for the future. However, it should never be the only reference point used. Examples can be found in every industry and field where organizations have been left in the dust as competitors surged ahead with breakthrough levels of performance. Setting goals based on the past is a strategy that will certainly lead to your eventual failure.

Arbitrary Stretch Goals

A number of today's leading-edge organizations have gone beyond setting goals strictly based on past performance. The new approach is called *stretch goals,* which require employees to rethink and reengineer work. Simply working harder will not allow a team to meet a stretch goal in most cases. I like stretch goals. I think they are a great way of forcing organizations to eliminate bureaucracy and unnecessary work. However, there is a smart way and a dumb way of setting stretch goals. The dumb way is to arbitrarily pick some number out of the air and establish it as a stretch goal. These kinds of goals are usually easy to spot, because they have nice round numbers like 10 or 100. I've seen a number of large corporations that have stretch goals like "tenfold improvement in product quality." When asked why 10, they respond by explaining that it is a nice round number that will require people to stretch to reach it.

One organization has an overall goal for every measure in the corporation called "80 in 5." This means that they want to see performance improve by 80 percent on all measures in five years. Motorola has received a lot of press for its "Six Sigma" goal, which calls for less than 3.4 defects per million products. Many companies now have their own six sigma goals that they have copied from Motorola. I worked with an electronics manufacturer that admired Motorola and established 3.4 defects per million as its goal. When asked how it was currently performing, I was told: "We're around 1,100 defects per million right now, but we used to be much worse." When asked why it selected 3.4 per million as the magic number, I was told that the fact that Motorola was in a similar business made it an appropriate goal. When Motorola set its goal of six sigma, it was based on thorough research of capabilities, past performance, and performance levels of key competitors. In other words, it did not just make up this number. The stretch goal was set based on research. However, this electronics company established it as the overall goal for every performance measure in the company. Six sigma is not required nor is the company willing to pay for this performance in all areas of business.

Establishing overall slogan type goals like "80 in 5" or "Six Sigma" is exactly the opposite of what I would like to see in a company's goal setting. Goals need to be based on the following:

- Past performance

- Competitor performance

- Performance of benchmark-level companies in similar businesses

- Analysis of technical capabilities and resource constraints

- Evidence that achievement of the goal/level will make the organization more competitive

- Feedback from employees and suppliers involved with the goal

- Analysis of how goal achievement may impact other measures.

One of the biggest problems with stretch goals set in an arbitrary fashion is that employees may not even try to achieve them, because they seem impossible. They know that senior management just made up the goal by pulling numbers out of the air, so it is unlikely that the goals will be supported. Rather than motivating employees to strive for break-through levels of performance, the stretch goal may cause them to give up trying.

Inconsistent Short- and Longer-Term Goals

When I evaluate organizations against the Malcolm Baldrige Award criteria, one of the factors I look for is inconsistencies between their annual business plans and their longer-term plans. What this means is that the performance measures on which goals are set in the annual plan are different from the measures on which long-term goals are based. For example, they have no short-term goal for sales to the Pacific Rim countries, but have a long-term goal for this. Or they have a short-term or annual goal for customer satisfaction levels, but no longer-term goal. Annual goals should be based on the exactly same measures as are longer-term goals. The annual goal should be a stepping stone to help reach the longer-term goal.

Ideally, the organization's plan should be laid out like that in Table 14.1. Notice that the longer-term goals and annual goals are all based on the same performance measures, and that the longer-term goals always call for a higher level of performance than the 1996 goal.

Inconsistencies in Goals at Different Levels of the Organization

A similar but different problem with organizational goals is that there are many disconnects across the different functions and levels in the organization. Engineering develops its own goals in isolation from its internal customers and suppliers. One business unit or location has completely different goals from other business units or locations that do the same things. These inconsistencies result because individual functions or locations do not base their goals on those above them, nor do they talk with each other when setting goals. These inconsistencies lead to major problems, because optimizing performance in one area often causes problems for another area.

TABLE 14.1   Annual and Longer-Term Goals

Measures	1996 Goals	1999 Goals
Customer-Related		
Percent increase in revenue from existing customers	5%	12%
Market share	26%	35%
Customer satisfaction survey	4.6/5.0	4.8/5.0
Complaints per 1000 orders	10	4
Employee-Related		
Turnover	15%	5%
Absenteeism	10%	6%
Employee satisfaction index	75%	85%
Stress index	68/100	80/100

The human resource department makes sure that every employee has goals stated in its annual performance plan. However, no one makes sure that these are the right goals or the right measures. The only way of really fixing this problem is to begin by redesigning performance measures for the entire company and then cascading this down through all levels and functions so that all have their own balanced scorecard of 10 to 20 measures of performance. Once you have a comprehensive set of measures that is consistent across all levels, short- and long-term goals need to be set in the same manner, in a top–down, bottom–up approach. Senior executives suggest goals for their direct reports, who challenge and discuss them until consensus is reached on reasonable goal levels. These same discussions then occur at all levels until goals have been written and agreed to by all levels of employees.

DEVELOPING STRATEGIES TO ACHIEVE YOUR GOALS

Setting goals is easy. I set a goal every year that I want to earn a million dollars; I have yet to reach it. Determining how to achieve your goals is the difficult part of the planning process. Obviously, I have not hit on an effective strategy for earning a million dollars a year. Once the goals have been agreed to for the macro performance levels in the organization, appropriate individuals need to be called together to develop strategies that will be used to achieve the goals. Usually, the one person who owns the measure will pull together a cross-functional team that will help develop strategies. For example, if one of the macro goals is to achieve a level of 80 percent employee satisfaction, the HR Vice President who owns this measure might call together a group of four to six other senior executives to help develop strategies or action plans for improving employee morale. Rarely is a single strategy used to achieve a goal. Most goals usually require a multifaceted strategy.

Developing strategies is often done by brainstorming ideas that could be considered for impacting performance on the measure. For example, if the goal is to achieve a level of 80 percent employee satisfaction, some of the strategies that might appear on the brainstorm list include the following:

- Job-sharing.
- Telecommuting.
- Parties/picnics.
- Improved safety efforts.
- Employee stock ownership program.
- 360-degree feedback appraisal system.
- Performance-based pay.
- Flextime.
- Recognition programs.
- Better benefits.
- Air conditioning in plants.
- More training.
- Increased empowerment.
- New equipment.

After brainstorming a list of possible strategies, each one is evaluated based upon predetermined criteria that usually include factors such as the following:

- Cost.

- Projected impact on measure/goal.

- Politics/culture.

- Time required to implement.

- Risk—chance of failure.

- Likelihood that management will approve.

The list of 15 to 20 possible strategies is then narrowed down to a reasonable number of perhaps four or five that will have the most impact, least cost, and the least risk. A separate project plan is then written for each strategy that specifies deliverables or products and the steps that will be used to complete the project. It is at this level of planning that it is alright to write project or activity goals. For example, an appropriate goal might be to "Design and implement telecommuting efforts in all corporate support functions where it is appropriate, by the end of 1996."

Strategies are often pilot-tested in a single unit or location before they are implemented across the organization. Each strategy needs to be evaluated based upon the impact it has on the appropriate performance measures. Sometimes, a single strategy will impact a number of performance measures, sometimes only one. Based on the results of the pilot, you will know whether to do a full-scale implementation or go back to the drawing board to look for a different strategy. Every failure brings a new lesson that should be communicated to others so they don't repeat your mistakes.

USING BENCHMARKING TO IMPROVE YOUR STRATEGIES

Benchmarking is one of the best methods of establishing realistic stretch goals and providing ideas for strategies to achieve your goals. Going to visit world-class companies that excel in areas where you are weak can be an enlightening experience that may save you years-worth of trial-and-error learning. The problem with benchmarking is that most companies don't do it correctly. Corporate field trips are often passed off as benchmarking, where employees wander around the benchmark organization, marveling at all its accomplishments, but never leaving with anything concrete. Benchmarking should only be done after identifying a performance measure and collecting data on your current level of performance on that measure. After finding out where you are with respect to suggestions per employee, real estate cost per square foot, or whatever the measure is, you need to spend time researching possible benchmark companies. Use multiple sources of data to find who is the best at the process or function you wish to benchmark and then do some investigation via telephone before buying airplane tickets for your team.

Once you select one or more organizations to benchmark, your mission should be to gather information to set an appropriate stretch goal for your own performance and to get ideas on strategies or approaches that you can apply in your own company. Borrowing the good ideas of others is what benchmarking is all about. This is how you can save a great deal of time and effort in coming up with good strategies. Rather than inventing your own, find out what has worked in other organizations and implement it in yours. The danger of this approach is that a strategy that worked well in one organization may bomb in your company. Before copying someone else's approach, make sure it will fit within the culture of your own business.

COMMUNICATING YOUR PLAN

I consulted with a company that would not let me review its strategic plan because it contained a great deal of confidential information that it would not want to leak to its competitors. Even though I had signed a nondisclosure agreement, the executives were leery of letting me read it. It turns out that the company also did not share the plan with any employees—they could not be trusted either, and really didn't need to know the overall company goals and strategies. Obviously, this is flawed logic. If employees don't know your goals and plans, they won't be able to help you reach them. Some companies have tried giving all employees a copy of their strategic plan binder and have been discouraged when most employees don't even skim it. Others realize that a 3-inch-thick plan will never be read, so they publish an abbreviated version on a wallet card that is handed out to all employees. I was giving a speech recently, joking about the wallet cards as a silly way of trying to communicate plans; more than half the audience held up their wallet cards. When I asked how many could recite what the card said without looking at it, only a few could. The problem with wallet cards is that they stay in the wallet or purse.

Employees need less than a 3-inch binder full of plans and probably more than a wallet card. They need to know the major performance measures and goals of the organization and the major strategies that will be used to achieve the goals. They also need to know how their functions and jobs fit in with the organization's goals. Every employee should be able to explain how his or her performance measures relate to those of the overall company. Communicating the plan one time is clearly a mistake, no matter what media or method is used. It just doesn't seem to sink in. Pacific Bell is a company that does a great job of communicating their four "Bold Goals" to employees by using a wide variety of media. Employees see the vision and bold goals every morning when they walk through the lobby, read about them in newsletters, hear about them in training programs and periodic meetings, and hear the goals discussed in periodic meetings where individual and team performance are reviewed. The key to the effectiveness of its communication is that much of it is personal—one on one between employee and supervisor or peer-level employees. Canned presentations or videos by themselves just don't seem to work well.

THE KEY TO SUCCESSFUL PLANS

To summarize what I have been saying about planning, here are 10 rules for making your plans effective:

1. Develop specific goals for each performance measure in your scorecard.

2. Identify annual and longer-term goals on the same measures.

3. Set stretch goals that are based on benchmarks and analysis of key competitors.

4. Develop goals and plans in a top–down, bottom–up fashion.

5. Make sure that goals are consistent across levels and functions.

6. Involve customers, key suppliers, and employees in the planning process.

7. Spend no more than six weeks each year preparing your plan; strive for no more than three drafts of the plan document.

8. Employ a systematic approach to select the best strategies for accomplishing your goals.

9. Use benchmarking to identify effective strategies for achieving your goals.

10. Communicate plans to all employees using a variety of methods and media, with more reliance on one-on-one communication than canned presentations.

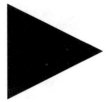

Bibliography

Bartlett, Christopher A., and Sumantra Ghoshal. "Changing the Role of Top Management: Beyond Strategy to Purpose." *Harvard Business Review,* November/December 1994.

Case, John. *Open Book Management—The Coming Business Revolution.* New York: Harper Business School Press, 1995.

Cortada, James W. "Balancing Performance Measurements and Quality." *Quality Digest,* December 1994.

Daniels, Aubrey. *Bringing Out the Best in People—How to Apply the Astonishing Power of Positive Reinforcement.* New York: McGraw-Hill, 1994.

Drucker, Peter F. "The Information Executives Truly Need." *Harvard Business Review,* January/February 1995.

Eccles, Robert G. "The Performance Measurement Manifesto." *Harvard Business Review,* January/February 1991.

Gale, Bradley T. *Managing Customer Value.* New York: The Free Press, 1994.

Gilbert, Thomas F. *Human Competence.* New York: McGraw-Hill, 1978.

Hamel, Gary, and C. K. Prahalad. *Competing for the Future.* Cambridge: Harvard Business School Press, 1994.

Heskett, J. L., T. O. Jones, G. W. Loveman, and W. E. Sasser. "Putting the Service-Profit Chain to Work." *Harvard Business Review,* March/April 1994.

Hronec, Steven. *Vital Signs—Using Quality, Time, and Cost Performance Measurement to Chart Your Company's Future.* New York: AMACOM Press, 1993.

Kaplan, Robert, and David Norton. "The Balanced Scorecard—Measures That Drive Performance." *Harvard Business Review,* January/February 1992.

———. "Putting the Balanced Scorecard to Work." *Harvard Business Review,* September/October 1993.

———. "Using the Balanced Scorecard as a Strategic Management System." *Harvard Business Review,* Jan/Feb, 1996.

Krulikowski, Claire. "Measuring Employee Satisfaction." *Quality Digest,* September 1994.

McTaggert, James M., Peter W. Kontes, and Michael C. Mankins. *The Value Imperative: Managing for Superior Shareholder Returns.* New York: The Free Press, 1994.

Montgomery, Cynthia A., and Michael E. Porter, (eds.). *Strategy: Seeking and Securing Competitive Advantage.* Cambridge: Harvard Business School Press, 1991.

Paré, Terance P. "The New Champ of Wealth Creation." *Fortune,* September 18, 1995.

Prahalad, C. K., and Gary Hamel. "The Core Competencies of the Corporation." *Harvard Business Review,* May/June 1990.

Rust, Roland T., Anthony J. Zahorik, and Timothy L. Keiningham. *Return on Quality—Measuring the Financial Impact of Your Company's Quest for Quality.* Probus Publishing, 1994.

Stewart, G. Bennett, III. *The Quest For Value—The EVA Management Guide.* New York: Harper Business School Press, 1991.

Thomas, Phillip R. *Competitiveness Through Total Cycle Time—An Overview for CEOs.* New York: McGraw-Hill, 1990.

Thor, Carl. *Measures of Success.* Essex Junction, VT: Oliver Wight Books, 1994.

Treacy, Michael, and Fred Wiersema. *The Discipline of Market Leaders.* New York: Addison-Wesley, 1995.

Tully, Shawn. "The Real Key to Creating Wealth." *Fortune,* September 20, 1993.

Zairi, Mohamed. *Measuring Performance for Business Results.* New York: Chapman & Hall, 1994.

Zuckerman, Marilyn R., and Lewis J. Hatala. *Incredibly American.* Milwaukee: ASQC Quality Press, 1992.

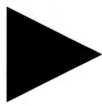

Index

ABC. See Activity-based costing
Accomplishment measurements, 23–25
Activity-based costing (ABC), 55–56, 91
Air Products and Chemicals, 107, 130, 142–43
Alcoa, 98
American Express, 45, 118
Arthur D. Little, 126
Assumptions, 60–61
AT&T, 4, 13, 43, 46, 52, 53, 78, 79–80, 130, 162

Baldrige Award, 27, 70, 102, 118–19, 130, 169
Behavior measurements, 23–25
Benchmarking, 188–89
Black & Decker, 83
Boeing, 45
Browning-Ferris Industries, 85–86
Business Incentives (co.), 134

Cargill, 116, 143–44, 146
Case, John, 176
"Chicken efficiency", 21–22
Ciba-Geigy, 5
Citicorp, 84
Client relationship index, 91–92
Coca-Cola, 43, 52, 53, 54, 116
Community service measurements, 33–34, 107–8
Comparative data, 173
Competence measurements, 22–23
Competition
  internal, 25–26
  price versus, 77–78
  process measurements of, 100–101
Complaints, 69

Coors Beer, 98
Cost of quality (COQ), 56–57, 105
Courtesy measurements, 22–23
Crosby, Phillip, 56, 105, 149
CSI. See Customer satisfaction, index
Customer(s)
  feedback, 62–64
  "hot-buttons", 60
  identification and classification, 59
  putting employees before, 123–24
  requirements, 6, 60–64, 84
  value, 43, 74–80
Customer satisfaction, 30, 43
  data, 64–67
  hard measurements, 67–70
  index, 70–72, 78–80
  internal, 72–74
  soft measurements, 64–68
  with suppliers, 114
Customer value index (CVI), 79
Cycle time, 101–2, 105–6

Data
  collection, 156–58
  comparative, 173
  customer satisfaction, 64–67
  detail, 17–19
  historical, 50–51
  performance, 171–78
  quantity, 16
  recent, 173
  reporting and analysis, 34–35
  scorecard, 41–42
  unnecessary, 173–74
Department of Motor Vehicles (DMV), 66–67, 101

Detail
    attention to, 84
    lack of, 17–19
DMV. *See* Department of Motor Vehicles
Documentation, 145–47
Domino's Pizza, 69, 101, 163
Downsizing, 125–26
Drucker, Peter, 51, 53

Economic value-added (EVA), 4, 6, 43, 52–54
Employee(s)
    before customers, 123–24
    intellectual capital of, 129–31
    measurements, 6, 30–31
    organizations and, 99–100
    productivity, 102–3
    requirements, 131–32
    safety, 33–34, 103–4, 106–7
    treatment of, 126–28
Employee satisfaction, 7–8, 45–46, 124–25
    hard measures, 136–37
    index, 7–8, 137–38
    profits and, 128–29
    soft measures, 134–36
    surveys, 132–33
Environmental measurements, 33–34, 107–8
ESI. *See* Employee satisfaction, index
EVA. *See* Economic value-added

Federal Express, 13, 46, 162, 169
Feedback, customer, 62–64
Financial measurements, 31, 42–43, 49–57
FMC Corporation, 142–43
Ford, 43
Future measurements, 5–6, 50–52, 108–9

Garbage quality, 85–86
Gayle, Bradley, 76, 80
General Electric, 54
Goals
    measurements and, 9–10, 163, 166–67,
        180–81
    mistakes setting, 181–86
    organizational, 185–86
    past performance, 182–83
    strategy and, 182, 186–88
    stretch, 183–85
    versus objectives and targets, 180–81
Growth measurements, 46–47

Hamel, Gary, 163
Hewlett-Packard, 84
Historical data, 50–51
Home Depot, 45, 129
Houghton, Jamie, 169
Hronec, Steve, 52, 161

IBM, 23–24, 43, 65, 121, 125, 177
Innovation measurements, 46–47
Intellectual capital, 129–31
ISO 9000 certification, 117–18, 182

Kaplan, Robert, 27, 108, 159, 161
Key success factors
    identification of, 148–50
    measurement and, 5, 164–68
    suppliers and, 119–20

Learning measurements, 46–47
Location measurements, 141, 142–44
Long-term goals, 185, 186

Management by objectives (MBO), 9, 182–83
Management hot buttons, 21–22
Market share, 69
Market value-added (MVA), 54–55
Mazda, 84
MBO. *See* Management by objectives
McDonald's, 83, 84, 100
Measurement(s)
    behavior versus accomplishments, 23–25
    benefits of, 12–13
    categories, 150–52
    competition versus teamwork, 25–26
    courtesy versus competence, 22–23
    customer, 6, 30, 43, 59–81
    deceiving, 167
    employee, 6, 30–31, 123–38
    environmental/public responsibility, 33–34,
        107–8
    financial, 31, 42–43, 49–57
    goals and, 9–10, 163, 166–67, 180–88
    key success factors, 5, 148–50, 164–68
    learning, innovation, and growth, 46–47
    model, 10–12
    operational, 31–32, 44, 95–110
    organizations, 6–7
    past, present, and future, 5–6, 50–52
    performance, 3–13, 19–22, 150

plan, 154–56
process, 44, 95–110
product/service quality, 33, 43–44, 85–93, 113
questionnaire, 28–37
relationships among, 176–77
safety, 33–34, 103–4, 106–7
score, 35–37, 41–47
shareholders, 6
short-term, 16–17
strategy and, 8–9, 10–12, 162–63
suppliers, 32, 44–45, 111–21
system
  characteristics, 4–10
  design, 141–58
  evaluation, 27–37
  problems, 15–26
time estimates, 158
top-down, 141–42, 143
unit/location, 141, 142–44
values and, 5, 43, 159–61, 168–69
vision and, 5, 159–63
vital versus trivial, 4–5, 152–53
Mercedes Benz, 104–5
Merck, 54
Microsoft, 54
Mission
definition of, 145
statement, 146, 159–62
Motorola, 118, 184
MVA. *See* Market value-added

New England Telephone, 130
Nordstrom, 22–23
Northrop Grumman, 10, 99, 135, 174–76
Norton, David, 27, 108, 159, 161

Objectives. *See* Goals
Odiorne, George, 9
Open-book management, 176
Operational measurements, 31–32, 44, 95–110
Organization(s)
employee, 99–100
goals of, 185–86
measurements, 6–7
score of, 41–47
Output measurements, 97–98
Outsourcing, 44–45
Owens Corning, 108, 109

Pacific Bell, 45, 107, 118, 135, 190
Past measurements, 5–6, 50–52
Past performance goals, 182–83
Performance
data, 171–78
measurement, 3–13, 19–22, 150
past, 182–83
Peters, Tom, 149
Pizza Hut, 163
Plan(s)
communication, 189–90
measurement, 154–56
successful, 190–91
Prahalad, C. K., 163
Present measurements, 5–6, 50–52
Price
and perceived value, 114–16
versus competition, 77–78
Process measurements, 44, 104–5
of competition, 100–101
cycle time, 101–2, 105–6
future-oriented, 108–9
productivity, 102–3
reasons for, 95–97
report card, 105–6
safety, 33–34, 103–4, 106–7
selection of, 98–99
selling, 23–25
of suppliers, 116–17
versus output, 97–98
Productivity, 102–3
Product/service quality, 33, 43–44, 83–93, 113
characteristics of, 86–89
customer requirements, 84
garbage, 85–86
index, 89–93
quantity and, 89
Profits
employee satisfaction and, 128–29
through downsizing, 125–26
Project team, 145
Publications, 20–21
Public responsibility measurements, 33–34, 107–8

Quaker Oats, 52, 53
Quality. *See* Product/service quality
Quantity measurements, 89

R&D function, 21, 103
Rework, 104–5
Ritz-Carlton, 84, 115–16
Rockwater (co.), 108–9, 161

Safety measurements, 33–34, 103–4, 106–7
Score
    calculation of, 35
    interpretation of, 36–37
    of organization, 41–47
Selling process, 23–25
Service quality. *See* Product/service quality
Short-term goals, 185, 186
Short-term measurements, 16–17
Situation analysis, 147–48
Smith, Fred, 162
Smithburg, William, 53
Solectron (co.), 70
Southwest Airlines, 129, 163
Speeches, 20–21
Springfield Remanufacturing Co., 176
Stack, John, 176
Stakeholders, 6, 72
Stern Stewart, 54
Stewart, G. Bennett III, 53
Strategy
    benchmarking and, 188–89
    development of, 162–63
    goals and, 182, 186–88
    measurements, 8–9, 10–12, 52, 162–63
    model, 10–12
Stretch goals, 183–85
Success factors. *See* Key success factors
Sundance Travel, 114–15
Supplier(s)
    customer satisfaction with, 114
    key business drivers and, 119–20
    management skills, 117–19
    measurements, 32, 44–45, 111–21
    price/value, 114–16
    processes, 116–17
    values regarding, 111–12, 114–16

Targets. *See* Goals
Teamwork, 25–26
Thomas, Philip, 101
Time estimates, 158
Top-down measurements, 141–42, 143
Total quality management (TQM), 12, 61
TQM. *See* Total quality management
Trivial measurements, 4–5, 152–53

United Airlines, 163
Unit measurements, 141, 142–44
University tenure point system, 20

Value(s)
    customer, 43, 74–80
    definition of, 146
    measurements and, 5, 43, 159–61, 168–69
    organization, 5, 159–61
    price, 114–16
    regarding suppliers, 111–12, 114–16
    statement, 147
Vision
    definition of, 146
    measurement and, 5, 159–63
    statement, 146–47, 159–62
Vital measurements, 4–5, 152–53

Wal-Mart, 54
Walt Disney, 84
Welch, Jack, 54
Writing, 19–20

Xerox, 23–24, 117

Yacura, Joe, 118
Yield, 104

Zenith, 98